Chocolate Peppers

ALSO BY TAB EDWARDS

Paper Problems (2006)
"Coffee is for Closers ONLY!" (2007)
I&O: Imaging & Output Strategy (2008)
MPS: Managed Print Services (2010)
Lessons of the Navel Orange (2011)
*Batman, Robin, David Beckham,
and the Naked King (2013)*

TAB EDWARDS

Chocolate Peppers

*Why Acting in Your
Own Self-Interest
is Good for You, Your
Loved Ones,
Society, and the World*

TMBE, PHILADELPHIA, PENNSYLVANIA 19129

TMBE

Copyright © 2014 by Tab M. Edwards. All rights reserved.

Printed in the United States of America. Except as permitted under the United States Copyright Act of 1976, no part of this publication may be reproduced or distributed in any form or by any means, or stored in a data base or retrieval system, without the prior written permission of the publisher.

ISBN 978-0-9700891-9-9

This publication is designed to provide authoritative information in regards to the subject matter covered. It is sold with the understanding that the publisher is not engaged in rendering legal, accounting, or other professional services. If legal advice or other expert assistance is required, the services of a competent professional person should be sought.

 —From a declaration of principles jointly adopted by a committee of the American Bar Association and a committee of publishers.

Tab Edwards books are available at special quantity discounts to use as premiums and promotions, or for use in corporate training programs. For more information, please visit the website TabEdwards.com.

Designed by Water Creative
Philadelphia, PA.

1 3 5 7 9 10 8 6 4 2

*To all those who dare
to act in their Self-Interest*

CONTENTS

INTRODUCTION 17

Chapter One:
THE $5,000 SUIT 30

Chapter Two:
THE JOYFUL RELIEF OF HAPPINESS 51

Chapter Three:
"WHY DID I BUY THAT SUIT?" /
WHY WE DO THINGS 61

Chapter Four:
THE GOODNESS OF SELF-INTEREST 75

Chapter Five:
"DAMN, I'VE GOTTA PEE." 104

Chapter Six:
RISK 140

Chapter Seven:
CHOCOLATE PEPPERS 151

Chapter Eight:
THE PEPPER TREE 161

Chapter Nine:
5 TIPS FOR ENJOYING YOURSELF *and* BEING BETTER 216

Chapter Ten:
THE CHAIN OF SELF-INTEREST LINKED: A SUMMARY 244

CONCLUSION 251

ABOUT THE AUTHOR 257

SELECTED BIBLIOGRAPHY 259

INDEX 273

Chocolate Peppers

"If you were free to do absolutely anything that you genuinely want or have ever wanted to do—*anything*—without penalty, without criticism, without concern for reputation, without repercussion, without loss, without any responsibilities, and—at your discretion—without anyone ever knowing about it, what would you do? Why haven't you done it?"

—Tab Edwards, Author

INTRODUCTION

THE IN-FLIGHT SAFETY DEMONSTRATION

If you have ever travelled by airplane, then—assuming you were paying attention—you have undoubtedly heard the announcement: "Ladies and gentlemen, my name is Jane and I'm your chief flight attendant. On behalf of Captain Smith and the entire crew, welcome aboard Fast Airlines Flight 123, non-stop service from Philadelphia to Los Angeles."

The announcement continues.

"Now we request your full attention as the flight attendants demonstrate the safety features of this aircraft." Then, after telling us to make sure our seat backs and tray tables are in their full upright position, that our seats belts are correctly fastened, and that we turn off any electronic equipment, the flight attendant eventually gets to the part of the safety demonstration that—when I first heard it—seemed counterintuitive: "Oxygen and air pressure are always being monitored. In the event of a decompression, an oxygen mask will automatically appear in front of you. To start the flow of oxygen, pull the mask towards you. Place it firmly over your nose and mouth, secure the elastic band behind your head, and breathe normally. Although the bag does not inflate, oxygen is flowing to the mask." Here's the kicker: "If you are traveling with a child or someone who requires assistance, secure your mask first, and then assist the other person. Keep your mask on until a uniformed crew member advises you to remove it."

" ... If you are traveling with a child ... secure your mask *first*"? So, I thought at the time, let me get this straight: I'm traveling with my kids and the airplane starts to malfunction, resulting in the loss of oxygen in the plane; no one can breathe. I look over at my kids and they are gasping for air. Although I have never actually experienced such an airplane malfunction, I have to believe that when faced with such a situation, I would panic and my nurturant instincts would inevitably kick in. Were this to happen, my primary concern would be the safety of my children. And, as a result, I would instinctively try to put *their* masks on first.

Of course, the experts on such matters all agree that my actions would jeopardize the safety of both me and my children. They argue that, in such an emergency, if I do not secure my own oxygen mask first, I will quickly lose my ability to deal with the emergency. The reason,

INTRODUCTION

they argue, is that, if there is a sudden loss of cabin pressure, I would probably only last 15 to 20 seconds without oxygen before losing consciousness. So it is very important that I can get my mask on quickly, giving me the ability to secure my children's masks. I would not be of any assistance to them if I passed out either before putting my mask on or after putting theirs on but before I've had a chance to put on mine.

That airplane scenario made me consider that, in some cases, by doing the thing that is in *my* best (self) interest (e.g. putting my oxygen mask on first) — regardless of how guilty or selfish engaging in the activity makes me feel — would not only be good for *me*, but also good for others (my children). Then I started thinking: If it's possible that doing something that is in my self-interest can be good for others, then what other actions or activities follow the same *good-for-me-good-for-others-too* pattern? Buying expensive clothing? Racing motorcycles? Eating "junk" food? Getting a college degree? Bungee jumping? Drinking vodka? Womanizing? Man-izing? Smoking crack cocaine? Going French (not showering)? Eating chocolate? And, if so, how could my act of *eating chocolate*, for instance, possibly be good for my family and friends? My mind was working over-time. And the more I thought about this slightly paradoxical notion, the more I started to believe — at least hypothetically — that in most, if not all, situations, the *good-for-me-good-for-others-too* linkage exists.

"I DETESTED THE TASTE OF ALCOHOL. But I needed its effects to exist in society," said Dr. Olivier Ameisen of his alcohol addiction. Ameisen, one of France's top heart specialists, had been professor of medicine at the Weill Medical College of Cornell University and is the author of the 2008 best-selling book *The End of My Addiction*. He says he tried every known remedy to end his dependence on alcohol—including nine months confined in clinics—but nothing worked. In 2000, he read an article about a man addicted to cocaine who was treated for muscle spasms with a muscle-relaxant called baclofen. The man found that the drug also eased his addiction to cocaine. Seeing how nothing else had worked in the treatment of his own alcohol addiction, Dr. Ameisen decided to experiment on himself and began self-administering doses of baclofen in March of 2002. According to Ameisen, he detected a lessening in his cravings for whiskey and gin almost immediately, and he was surprised that baclofen was unknown to specialists on dependence. He wrote that, of the "anti-craving medications used in animals, only one—baclofen—has the unique property of suppressing the motivation to consume cocaine, heroin, alcohol, nicotine and d-amphetamine. The effect is dose-dependent."

According to the National Institute on Alcohol Abuse and Alcoholism, about 18 million people in the United States have an alcohol use disorder—a medical condition diagnosed when a person's drinking causes distress or harm, classified as either alcohol dependence (alcoholism) or alcohol abuse. For these 18 million people (5%

of the U.S. population), there is the promise of a possible solution to their problem of alcohol dependence. And that doesn't even include the millions of people who are addicted to other substances like cocaine and heroin. This breakthrough is owed to Olivier Ameisen who, in an attempt to cure himself of his addiction to alcohol, discovered something that millions of other people around the world can benefit from, too.

This is another example of how someone acting in his self-interest engaged in an activity that turned out to be good for himself (freedom from an alcohol addiction), his loved ones (no longer having to support an alcoholic), society (he can provide better care for his patients and has helped millions with their addictions), and the world (fewer people addicted to destructive substances who are, therefore, more productive). And it's because of situations like this—and the airline flight instructions—that I began to suppose that a person acting in his or her self-interest could benefit other people and, ultimately, have a positive impact on the world.

My Self-Interest Supposition

Self-Interest Action ▶ Benefits the Actor ▶ Benefits Others ▶ the Common Good ▶ a Better World

After considering the positive impact that a singular person can have on others, I began to explore my supposition further: If we act in our own self-interest, it's likely that the result of our action will ultimately have a positive impact on those with whom we have an immediate relationship and on the broader society in general. And if there does exist such a relationship between doing what is in our self-interest and a resulting positive outcome on society, then shouldn't we simply do what we believe to be in our self-interest? Put more simply, shouldn't we just capitulate to our own instinct of doing whatever we believe will bring us gratification—based on the assumption that whatever brings us this gratification is, by extension, helping the greater good?

But acting in our own self-interest is not as easy as it may sound. Not because the activities in which we wish to engage are necessarily difficult or out of reach, but because of the external influences on our decisions. If left to our own devices without any external pressures—such as nagging, punishment, penalty, public opinion, feeling ostracized, or the fear of eternal damnation—I believe we would engage in more activities that bring us pleasure and make us happy, than those activities we engage in simply because we are otherwise influenced to do so. Even if we exclude the understandable external influences of physical punishment and legal and financial penalty, our behaviors are still overwhelmingly influenced by public opinion. Because we care far too much about what other people think of us and how people will judge our behaviors, we engage in activities that, absent

INTRODUCTION

this influence, we wouldn't do so otherwise. Instead, we would act in our self-interest and only engage in those activities in which we *want* to engage because the activities provide convenience, satisfy a need, bring us pleasure, or make us happier and more fulfilled.

Imagine waking up on a Saturday morning when you have absolutely nothing to do; no reason to go outside, no dog to walk, no lawn to mow, no kids' soccer practice, no honey-do list, no relatives to visit, no birthday parties, no shopping to do, no people to see, *nothing*! What would you do? Would you bathe? Would you comb your hair? Would you put on any clothing? Would you change out of your pajamas? What would you wear? Would you put on a business suit with a necktie or would you, instead, go business-casual? If fortunate enough to ever have such a nothing-to-do-Saturday, most people would wear "comfortable" clothing—if they wore anything—such as jeans, a t-shirt, or sweat gear; or they would wear loungewear, such as shorts, pajamas, a robe, boxer shorts, an A-shirt (tank top t-shirt), or that raggedy garment they have owned since high school. Why? Because these clothing choices allow the wearer to feel physically comfortable and that comfort provides us with pleasure. And if no one was going to see you on that nothing-to-do-Saturday, then there would be no one to frown upon your choice of clothing and make you feel embarrassed about wearing it. This suggests that the primary reason, if not the only reason, why we wear "presentable" clothing is so we can gain the approval of others. We want to know that our choice of clothing is satisfactory based on some arbitrary standard of acceptability. We don't wear the "presentable" clothing for ourselves—if we acted of our own volition, we would wear our most comfortable, dirty, nothing-to-do-Saturday clothing all the time—but, instead, we wear them because of other peoples' opinions of us.

So, I ask again: on that nothing-to-do-Saturday, would you bathe? Tell the truth. If you answered "yes," why? Eighty percent of people in the United States claim they bathe every day, and the primary reason why people bathe is because of the social repercussions that result from smelling "bad." On nothing-to-do-Saturdays, the percentage of people who bathe could be as much as 50% fewer. The reason? If people had no expectation of seeing or being around other people (except, perhaps, immediate family members who couldn't care less or will at least give us a pass about how badly we look or smell), there would be no risk of damage to our reputation for stinking and, therefore, no reason to bathe on that Saturday. And when you consider that there are benefits of not bathing every day: the retention of the skin's natural oils which reduces dry skin and eczema; the retention of skin bacteria that produce antibiotics which kill off bad bacteria; and water conservation; it stands to reason that foregoing that daily shower could be a good thing. So we bathe every day for the same reason why we don't wear pajamas and dirty loungewear to our kids' schoolmates' birthday parties: other people's opinions of us.

INTRODUCTION

And it doesn't stop there. Women: do you *really* want to shave your armpits every couple of days? Probably not, but most likely you do. Why? Sleeveless dresses! When women began wearing sleeveless dresses circa 1915, an advertisement in *Harper's Bazaar* fashion magazine advised that women who wore the sleeveless dress should see to "the removal of objectionable hair" from their armpits. Why? Because other people would see the risqué underarm hair and might assume you are Annie Jones, the hairy P. T. Barnum circus attraction. Eventually your socially unacceptable underarm hair would encourage the to-shave-is-to-be-feminine-believing public to form a hygienically unfavorable opinion of you. And no woman would encourage that opinion. So what do women do? Shave their armpits! But if you were lounging at home on that nothing-to-do-Saturday, shaving your armpits would not even be a consideration.

To quote actor and comedian Drew Carey as he explained the point-scoring system of his ABC improvisational comedy "Whose Line is it Anyway?": "The points are just like soap in the men's room. Doesn't matter." Most men won't admit it, but many of us don't wash our hands after using a public bathroom. In a nationwide poll conducted by Harris Interactive, 75% of the adult men surveyed claimed that they washed their hands after using a public bathroom. However, when these same respondents were actually observed in the bathroom, the percentage fell by approximately 10%. One estimate from a different study showed that when men are *alone* in a public bathroom, we wash our hands only 30% of the time. Why do we wash our hands at a higher percentage when other people are in the bathroom with us than we do when we are by ourselves in the bathroom? The answer: Because of the way we will be perceived by others if we don't wash our hands.

The common thread running through each of these examples is the fact that we very often do things (like shave our armpits) not because we genuinely *want* to do them, but because we fear and care too much about what other people will think of us if we did not do these things. A research study published in the journal *Current Biology* found that there is a biological reason for social conformity which explains why the opinions of others can affect our decisions, behaviors, and how much we value our possessions. Basically, the findings suggest that conformity and the opinions of others activates the same brain function as does receiving a reward, meaning that the more a person is influenced by the opinions of others, the greater the "reward" experience.

There is also a psychological explanation for why we are so easily influenced by and care so much about other people's opinions of us. In his 1943 paper "A Theory of Human Motivation," psychologist Abraham Maslow introduced his concept of a hierarchy of needs in which he argued that our physiological needs, security needs, social needs, esteem needs, and self-actualizing needs play a major role in motivating our behavior. Based on Maslow's hierarchy of needs, the approval of others (and thus, their opinions of us) gives us a higher sense of self-worth and satisfies our need for the respect of others. It is believed that the approval of others plays a role in how we value ourselves and in our determination of our own self-worth—our self-esteem need.

So while we may always *want* to act in our self-interest, it is not always easy to do because we care a little too much about what other people think of us. But, as I will make the case throughout this book, it is not only in our own best (self) interest to do whatever the hell we want to do, but is also ultimately good for our friends, family, community, society, and the world. The challenge is: How do we overcome external influences on our behaviors (such as our fear of having other people form unfavorable opinions of us) and make the decision to do the things that we genuinely *want* to do, as opposed to those things that we only do because we are being *influenced* to do them? Overcoming this challenge can unlock the doors to increased levels of satisfaction, happiness, and fulfillment. It will also curtail our utterance of five of the most depressing, resentful, saddest words a person could ever string together: *Damn! I wish I woulda*.

External influences on one's behavior can come from a variety of sources, including friends, relatives, teachers, co-workers, club members, and even one's religion. In Catholicism—the religion in which I was raised—for instance, divorce goes against the teachings of the religion and is strongly frowned upon. Therefore, to practicing Catholics and those of other religious faiths, when you get married, you remain married forever. And if you have marital problems, you and your spouse are encouraged to seek counseling and work through your differences.

We often hear about tragic situations where a married woman is in an unhealthy, physically abusive relationship but is motivated to endure the abuse because the woman's religious customs (the external influence) compel her to stay with her abusive spouse. To the abused woman, divorce is not seen as an option, and as a result, the woman remains in the relationship, the type of relationship which often ends tragically. In such relationships, the woman may *want* to act in her self-interest and leave the abusive husband (although leaving an abusive relationship is no guarantee of safety), but because of the external influence of the woman's religion and its teachings, the woman may feel compelled to stay in the relationship (which is guaranteed *not* to be safe). At some point—perhaps after the woman has unfortunately become the victim of serious injury at the hands of her abusive husband—the woman might find the strength and courage to escape the relationship and begin the next chapter of her life. And when she does she will undoubtedly look back on the relationship and think: "Damn! I wish I woulda left that abusive a**hole years earlier!"

Other external influences on our decisions are neither as strong nor as compelling as those exerted by one's faith or beliefs. Influences as flimsy as our friends' opinions can lead us to make decisions which we otherwise would not have made if we acted in our self-interest. As a single person, for instance, what if you saw the most beautiful man or woman you have ever laid eyes on—the type of person you have always *dreamed* about meeting—

sitting all alone in a coffee shop, periodically sending inviting glances and smiles your way? But, because your friends think the person is unattractive, they discourage you from introducing yourself to the person. Eventually, after sensing no interest from you, the beautiful person leaves the coffee shop, leaving you to wonder about the possibilities and what could have been. If this happened to you, I'm sure you would be thinking: "Damn! I wish I woulda ignored my friends and introduced myself to what might have been my future spouse."

A while back, I saw what was possibly the most beautiful men's suit I had ever seen. Every day since I first saw the suit, I dreamed of what it would be like to actually own and wear that beautiful suit; I couldn't stop thinking about it. And the fact that I could not find the suit in my size only made my desire for the suit grow even stronger. Oh, and did I mention that the suit cost more than $5,000? Then one day—to my surprise and delight—I found the suit in my size! At that point I had a decision to make: do I succumb to external influence and use the $5,000 to build my kids' college fund or do I act in my own self-interest, say "forget the kids, let them fend for themselves" and purchase the suit? It was not an easy decision.

CHAPTER

THE $5,000 SUIT

01

As hedonistic and wasteful as it may sound, I'll admit it: I once bought a $5,495 business suit. And to make matters worse, I also bought a pair of $1,000 Vass shoes. I know… I know… I know, that's a bit excessive, considering I could have just as easily gone to The Men's Wearhouse and purchased an attractive suit that would serve the same basic purpose for less than one-tenth of the price. Yes, I did take that into consideration. But you have to understand—the suit is simply *beautiful*! And when I put it on I feel like a million bucks! And the shoes? *Fuhgeddaboudit*.

When contemplating that suit purchase, the decision wasn't easy; I wrestled with it for a quite a while:

ME: "Wow. That's an absolutely beautiful suit."

MY INNER-SELF: "Yes, it is."

ME: "I bet it'd look great on me!"

MY INNER-SELF: "Yep. Probably would."

ME: "I wonder how much it costs."

MIS: "Well, if you have to ask, then you can't afford it."

ME: (Looking at the price tag). "$5,500 dollars?! Damn!"

MIS: "'Damn!' is right!"

ME: "But I've wanted a suit like this for years!"

MIS: "And you actually survived without it."

ME: "Hmm. Should I buy the suit or not?"

MIS: "Well, that depends. Do you *need* the suit?"

ME: "Well, no, I don't *need* the suit; I have several other perfectly fine suits that I can wear. But I really *want* to own *this one*. It's exceptional!"

MIS: "How badly would you feel if you didn't buy the suit today, went home to sleep on it, and returned tomorrow only to find that the suit had been sold and there were no other suits of that type available in your size?"

ME: "I would be really disappointed, I would kick myself every day, and I would think: 'Damn! I wish I woulda purchased the suit when I had the chance.'"

MIS: "Then why don't you go ahead and buy the suit?"

ME: "Because $5,000 is a lot of money to spend on a suit, and there are so many other things I could do with that money."

MIS: "No sh*t."

ME: "Besides, I would feel guilty spending $5,000 on a suit that I don't really *need*."

MIS: "Okay, then *don't* buy the suit. Spare yourself the guilt and use the $5,000 for those other things the money can be used for."

ME: "But, Inner-Self, you just don't understand. I have been looking for that particular suit for several months and I finally found one in my size. To walk away from it now would be my *Casablanca*/'We'll always have Paris' moment."

MIS: "Well, Tab, since you want to talk in *movie quotes*, then I suggest you channel your inner Curtis 'Miles' Armstrong from the 1983 film *Risky Business* and tell yourself: 'Sometimes you've just gotta say *what the f**k!*' and buy the suit."

And that's exactly what I did: I bought the suit ... *and* the shoes.

That summer I was invited to be the Keynote Speaker at the national sales meeting for a *Fortune 500*® corporation. I wore *the suit*. As I launched into my talk, I noticed something interesting—I felt *great*! Don't get me wrong, I always feel good when I'm on stage in front of an audience, but on this day I felt atypically good. After speaking to the assembled audience for a few minutes, it suddenly hit me: it wasn't just my words that transferred to the audience, but my confidence as well—confidence I felt because I wore the $5,000 suit! The fit was perfect, the drape was nearly flawless, and the suit moved with me; it was super comfortable. That beautiful, insanely-overpriced suit made me believe that it *looked* great on me. And because I believed that the suit looked great on me, I started believing that some of the suit's attractiveness would rub off on me and increase the overall attractiveness of my packaging. I started believing that if the audience took notice of the suit's attractiveness, they might say to themselves, "Wow! That's a great suit! If he can afford a suit like *that* he must get hired quite often to do speaking engagements. And if he gets hired often to speak at these types of events, then he must really know his stuff. And because he really knows his stuff, I'm going to pay close attention to what he's saying because it might help me become a better sales representative."

That belief—whether justified or not—gave me an added level of confidence on stage, and that added confidence served to enhance my performance. And my enhanced performance enabled me to more effectively communicate my message to the audience which—as I was later informed by a company executive—inspired the audience members to work at becoming better, more effective professionals. And many of them succeeded.

Those audience members who were motivated by my talk and worked to become better at their jobs, were also able to improve their work performance and earn more money. By improving their work performance, they helped the company improve its overall financial performance which enabled the company to grow and hire more people. As the company hired more people, it helped lift some families out of poverty and—both directly and indirectly—contributed money back into the economy. With more money flowing through the economy, the economy got stronger and even more people benefited from the economic prosperity. And it was all because one day I decided to spend $5,000 on a suit!

The conjunction of (A) My curiosity about whether taking care of yourself *first* as a recipe for the betterment of one's self and others applies to other situations, and; (B) The airplane flight instruction, the Olivier Ameisen experience, and my speaking engagement experience (in which wearing the $5,000 suit helped me to perform better—resulting in the audience being motivated to perform better) led me to formulate a hypothesis that taking care of yourself first and doing what's in your self-interest is not only good for you, but is also ultimately beneficial to other people. And if that is a valid assumption, then acting in your self-interest will have a positive impact on society in general, and ultimately, the world. I refer to this self-interest supposition as **The Chain of Self-Interest**.

The Chain of Self-Interest

As I describe in greater detail in Chapter Four: *The Goodness of Self-Interest* and throughout the remainder of this book, I believe that positive relationships and correlations such as that between my purchase of the suit and the resulting benefits to me, other people, society, and the world do exist. The Chain of Self-Interest began with my purchase of the $5,000 suit and developed like this:

1. Something compelled me to purchase a suit; possibly an *esteem need* (more about that later)
2. I purchased a long-sought-after suit and the purchase gave me pleasure
3. The suit looked good and it made me feel good; it also gave me more confidence
4. When I feel good I'm happier
5. When I'm happy, my happiness spreads to other people
6. When I'm happy, I also perform better
7. When I perform better, I am able to engage with the audience more effectively
8. When I engage with an audience more effectively, it helps them to get inspired
9. When they get inspired, their performance improves
10. When their performance improves, they make more money and are happier

11. When they are happy, they are more productive
12. When their productivity increases, their company's financial performance improves
13. When the company's financial performance improves, the company can hire more people
14. When the company hires more people, more people have more disposable income and spend more money
15. When people spend more money, the overall economy improves
16. When the economy improves, peoples' general standard of living improves
17. When peoples' general condition improves, they are happier
18. When people are happy, they spread happiness to other people
19. When people are happy, they become more cooperative
20. When people are more cooperative, they are more productive
21. When people are more productive, societies improve
22. When societies improve, the world is a better place
23. My $5,000 suit purchase helped make the world a better place

THE $5,000 SUIT

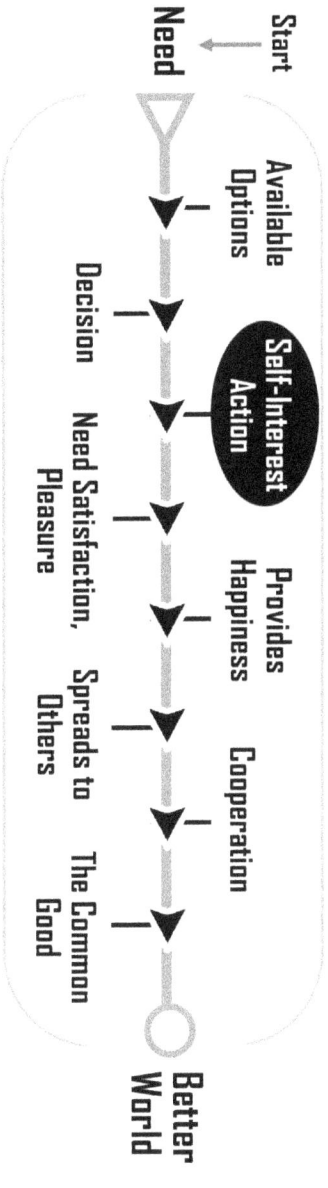

The Chain of Self-Interest for my purchase of the $5,000 suit is illustrated below:

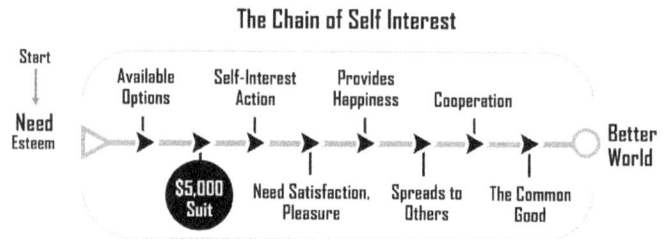

Okay, maybe this egocentric assessment of the impact that my purchase of an overpriced suit had on the goodness of the world is a bit accentuated; in the chain of self-interest illustrated above, the suit is merely a symbol. However, as I will make my case throughout this book, The Chain of Self-Interest—the general idea that a person acting in his or her self-interest can influence the betterment of others and society in general—is not at all far-fetched. Consider this: Suppose that you are preparing to cook a pot of beans. You use a pot, 32 ounces of water, and a one-pound bag of beans. If the pot weighs two pounds, and the water weighs two pounds, and the beans weigh one pound, then the entire bean adventure would weigh five pounds (2 + 2 + 1 = 5). Now suppose that you want to season the beans, so you add one single grain of pepper—that's right, one grain of pepper—and that grain of pepper weighs 0.000010582 ounces. Since the grain of pepper has mass and weight—regardless of how minuscule—the addition of the pepper would increase the overall weight of the bean adventure by the weight of the pepper, thus increasing the overall weight to 5 pounds and 0.000010582 ounces.

The Impact of "More"

If we applied this same logic to my purchase of the suit and the resulting impact on the goodness of the world, it stands to reason that any amount of happiness and increased productivity that are directly attributable to my purchase of the suit would have a positive impact on the world. In this case, the world is the pot, the people are the water, and the beans are people's productivity and happiness. If my purchase of the suit only contributes a measly 0.000010582 ounces of happiness to the world (the grain of pepper), then—mathematically, physically, and logically—the overall amount of happiness in the world must increase by 0.000010582 happy ounces. And if the total amount of world happiness increases—even minimally—then the total amount of world cooperation and productivity would increase. And if total world productivity increases, people would make new discoveries and develop new solutions to problems, ultimately resulting in even more happy and healthy people, as well as societal advancement. And when people are happier, healthier, and societies advance, the world becomes a better place.

Yes, I get how outlandish and self-congratulating this sounds. But what is by no means exaggerated is the fact that the suit made me feel more confident and comfortable than I normally felt in a suit. And since people attribute *credibility* to confident people, and credible people are more impactful and effective at motivating people to a specific course of action, the added credibility helped me to more effectively inspire the audience members to excel. And, in turn, the audience members' excellence contributed to the accomplishment of the goal and objectives which I was engaged to support.

While my sense of added confidence was fundamentally derived from my belief that the audience found my *suit* to be attractive, the unflattering reality is more likely that—deep down inside—I believed the audience's perception of my *suit* somehow spread to me and, therefore, contributed to the audience perceiving *me* (my overall packaging) as being more attractive. And, as studies have shown, a person's attractiveness garners more favorable opinion and treatment for that person. So that belief, on my behalf, is likely what gave me the added confidence to perform better.

The idea that a person's "packaging" or overall general attractiveness—whether enhanced by their clothing, haircut, style, vibe, or personality—can help improve the person's performance, is not such a far-fetched idea. In fact, author and personal branding strategist Catherine Kaputa goes so far as to suggest that a person's clothing will help how that person's performance is perceived by an audience. I believe that when I wore that suit it made me feel good and it helped improve my overall packaging which, in turn, improved my overall effectiveness with the audience, which contributed to a successful speaking engagement.

My belief that a person's perceived attractiveness can garner that person favorable opinion and treatment is supported by research. The term "judgmental bias" refers to situations in which one's judgments of a person's quality or character can be influenced by one's overall impression of that person. For example, if a person considers someone to be attractive, the person will attribute other positive qualities to the attractive person, such as intelligence, friendliness, likability, and the ability to display good judgment. And in these studies, these qualities are less likely to be attributed to a less attractive person. This bias, also known as the "Halo Effect," suggests that attractive people are treated differently because we live in a culture that places a high premium on external appearance. And this favorable treatment has also been shown to be a contributing factor in the attractive person's success.

A study published in *The Journal of Economic Psychology* found that attractive people tend to be more successful because they can generate cooperation among co-workers more easily than less attractive people. And a study published in *The American Economic Review* even found that attractive, or "good-looking," people earn more money than average-looking people who earn more money than plain people.

This entire discussion of the impact of one's attractiveness begs the question: What is an "attractive," "good-looking," or "beautiful" person anyway?

A "good-looking" person refers to a person whose physical characteristics (for instance, face, body, height, weight—*looks*) we find pleasing. In this context, "good-looking" is synonymous with "attractive" in the sense that we are attracted to people we believe possess these attributes. And "beauty"? Well, it lays in the opinion of the person who perceives it during a specific period in time. What I mean by this is if you asked a person to define a female standard of beauty in, say, 19th century America, the person would likely describe someone who is Rubenesque (plump, or having a physique associated with Flemish painter Peter Paul Rubens' portraits of women). In the 21st century, however, the preference seems to be for women on the slimmer end of the spectrum. In addition, what Bob considers beautiful, Ken might consider unattractive. So while there is no particular agreement on what constitutes "beauty," there is evidence that, within a given culture at a given point in time, there is agreement on the standards of beauty.

If, for instance, 100 people were asked to rank the appearances of people in a photograph based on a range of rating options (such as very handsome/beautiful; above average/good-looking; homely, etc.), the people's ratings of the subjects' appearance would be consistent. In other words, most of the 100 people would agree on which people in the photo were considered to be "beautiful," which people were considered to be "good-looking," and which people were considered to be "homely," even though the 100 people would be unable to agree on why they rated them as such.

Thinking back to the good feeling and added level of confidence I felt when I wore that $5,000 suit, it was probably born of the notion that I believed my perception of "attractiveness" was more than likely consistent with the perception of "attractiveness" on the part of my audience. And, therefore, since I believed that the *suit's* attractiveness had rubbed off on me and made *me* more attractive, so, too, would the audience, and that made me feel more confident.

"How'd He Get *HER*?!"

In her 1878 book *Molly Bawn*, Margaret Wolfe Hungerford wrote that "beauty is in the eye of the beholder." In the context of this discussion, Hungerford's statement raises the following question: In order for a person's beauty, good looks, clothing, or other accoutrements to help a person's performance or how a person's performance is perceived by an audience, wouldn't the audience base that person's overall packaging on their subjective standards? And since one person's attractiveness is another person's *opinion*, isn't believing that a performance is improved based on this assumption of attractiveness just a crap-shoot? After all, what if the beholder doesn't find a person's packaging "attractive"—even though the *person* believes it is? This is a fair point to consider, especially since what we *think* might aid in our attractiveness (my suit, for example) could be wildly off target when compared to another person's perception of our attractiveness.

Is actress Salli Richardson attractive? Actor Brad Pitt? Actress Eva Mendes? Italian actress Sophia Loren (in her prime)? Actor Shemar Moore? 1960's super model Jean Shrimpton? Model Alek Wek? If your answers to these questions is "yes", you are probably basing your answers on the person's *looks* (physical characteristics such as face, body, etc.). But, in actuality, we form our opinions of a person's attractiveness based on an *overall package*. And when we do, a person's physical characteristics or good looks can be less significant factors when determining their "attractiveness" than some other characteristic or attribute. Consider the case of an old friend of mine named "Tim."

At some point in our lives we've all said it or thought it. Whenever we see a 5'2" tall decidedly nondescript— if not outright "ugly"— guy walking hand-in-hand with a stunning 6-foot tall supermodel, we scratch our heads and wonder: How'd he get HER?! And, at that point, our imagination takes over and we begin to rationalize how such a troll could possibly land a beautiful woman like that. I say we "rationalize" because—let's face it—the thoughts that we come up with (he's rich, she's desperate …) are designed to make us feel better about *ourselves* in light of the fact that *we* can't get a supermodel! But, in the end, I think it boils down to the likelihood that the troll just has "It." What is "It"? "It" is whatever the supermodel was looking for at the time she met the troll, and the troll gave her the assurance that he could deliver "It." But one thing is certain: the "It" most certainly is not the troll's physical characteristics or good looks.

Although I've witnessed the troll-supermodel enigma numerous times over the years, there is one guy I consider the poster-child for "How'd he get HER?!" His name is "Tim"—"Ugly Tim" as we, his friends, call him. Yes, Tim is admittedly UGLY! There are no two ways about it. How ugly? Rumor has it that when he was born his mother took one look at him and said, "It's okay, I'll love him anyway."

But some things about Tim *are* appealing: he has the "gift of gab," he's well-read, he dresses nicely, he listens attentively, and he understands the human psyche. For instance, Tim was once in a local dating competition where he was competing against two other men for the affections of one woman. It was similar to the 1960's television show *The Dating Game*, where a woman asked three men (who were hidden behind a wall so that the woman couldn't see what they looked like) a series of questions and, based on their answers, she chose one of the men to go out on a date with her. At Tim's competition, when the three men came out onto the stage, the crowd began snickering when Tim walked out. And when he introduced himself, the crowd began to boo; he was obviously not the crowd favorite. He was short and ugly, but I must admit: he was wearing the most flattering Ozwald Boateng suit I had ever seen!

So the show began and the bachelorette started asking the three men various questions. It became obvious after the third question or so that Tim was a man of substance and was somehow able to say all the right things in response to the bachelorette's questions. And the audience loved his answers! So much so, that by the end of the show, Tim had won over the crowd and was ultimately selected by the bachelorette. And when Tim walked out from behind the wall to meet the bachelorette, she took to him like he was *Brad Pitt* and not Ugly Tim!

Something else we say whenever a short, Tim-ugly guy is seen walking with a gorgeous super-model: "He has to either be physically well-endowed or rich." But even if he was physically well-endowed, he still had to, at some point, approach the supermodel, get her to talk to him, and then hold her interest before she had the chance to be turned-off by his looks. I sincerely doubt that he just walked up to her and said, "Hi, I'm Tim," and then *whipped it out*! And if he had money, same thing: I doubt that he simply walked up to her and said, "Hi, I'm Tim. Want some money?" No, the truth is that, whatever his circumstances, Ugly Tim had to approach a total stranger and sell himself as someone she'd want to hang out with. And that always begins with an initial conversation, a conversation that I'm certain would be easier to initiate if Tim was more handsome. It's like the

Greek philosopher Aristotle said: Personal beauty is a better introduction than any letter.

There are times when an "Ugly Tim" may be famous and/or has a reputation that precedes him, thus facilitating his introduction to beautiful women. If this was the case, it would make the "Ugly Tim's" connection with a supermodel much easier. But famous people only account for about 2% of the population, which means that 98% of the time, Tim is starting from scratch. But I've seen him in action many times, and it's something to behold!

One evening Tim and I were with some friends in a Philadelphia nightclub. As guys often do, we scouted the joint for the most attractive women. Although there were many in attendance that night, none caught our attention more than this one ravishing woman with movie-star good looks (yes, we were shallow back then). There we were: Four quasi-successful, well-educated bachelors who were ALL reluctant to approach this woman—all, that is, except Ugly Tim. Tim was fearless, and the fear of rejection was not in his DNA.

"Excuse me, fellas," he said, as he left our group and walked toward the gorgeous woman. He approached the woman and tapped her on the shoulder. When she turned around to see who it was, we all saw the look of sheer disgust and disappointment come over her face, as if she was thinking: "Eew! I *know* your ugly ass is not trying to talk to ME!" But then something inexplicable happened. Tim politely apologized for disturbing her, whispered something into her ear, and—like magic—

the woman started blushing and laughing! They talked for a few more minutes and then Tim grabbed her by the hand and escorted her over to our table! (Huh!?). He asked her to join us, and we all just sat in amazement as Tim went to work. It was masterful!

It was revealed that this woman was Scandinavian, and Tim would ask her questions such as: "Are you in support of all of the press that Lene Gammelgaard has been receiving for being the first Scandinavian woman to reach the peak of Mount Everest, or are you saddened that such exposure is commercializing Everest and tempting other women with a potential danger?" (What!?) We all had absolutely no clue what Tim was talking about, but the woman responded with awe. "Oh my gosh! Lene Gammelgaard is my HERO ...!" It was amazing. And as the woman spoke, Tim just listened intently and appeared to genuinely absorb every word the woman was saying. It was an interesting pattern: Tim would ask a question, the woman would talk for several minutes as Tim listened, and then Tim would respond with another, equally poignant, question.

Periodically, Tim would check with the woman to make sure she was comfortable and would buy her drinks or snacks if she wanted, and then the conversation would continue. After about forty-five minutes of listening to Tim and the woman chat like school-mates, I noticed that the woman was beginning to take in other aspects of the overall Tim package. She would comment on how great his suit was, how sweet he was, and how much fun she was having with him. By this point, my friends and

I had had enough and decided to leave the nightclub, allowing Tim the chance to enjoy his amazing conquest.

The next day I bumped into Tim and the woman at a shopping mall; they were holding hands like a couple of newlyweds! And almost everyone that passed them would look at them with an expression on their face that screamed: How'd he get HER?!

As Tim proved, it's not always a person's physical good looks that attract people to them, but is more likely the person's overall likability quotient, or "Q-rating" as they say in T.V. land. And a person's likability relates more to the person's *overall package*—what's on the inside as well as the outside—than to a person's physical appearance alone. A person's confidence, conversational skills, and knowledge can have a significant impact on how they are perceived by others. And if this perception is favorable, as I wrote previously, the favorable perception can contribute to a person's improved performance, which can increase a person's self-esteem, which can contribute to a person's happiness, which can spread and impact others, which can spread and impact the world.

There is evidence that supports the notion that something as simple as a pleasure-inducing purchase of a suit can contribute to a person's happiness and performance, as it did in my case. And when someone is happy and fulfilled they tend to be healthier and live longer; they also tend to be more self-confident, more cooperative, more productive, and more successful. A person's happiness spreads to other people who, in turn, derive these same benefits from being happy. And when people are more cooperative, they tend to be more productive; this contributes to advancement and new developments, all of which contribute to the greater common good.

Consider this: if enough people engaged in self-considering, pleasure-inducing acts (e.g. purchasing a suit, buying a pair of shoes, ordering lobster, eating donuts, having sex, coaching little league, or contributing to a charity), their happiness would spread to other people, whose happiness would spread to even more people, and so on. And as people are more fulfilled, society as a whole benefits from a healthier, more productive, more cooperative, more successful community of people until, ultimately, the world is a better place.

So, in a sense, by saying, "What the f**k!" and acting in my self-interest to purchase the $5,000 suit, that self-interested behavior—irrespective of how financially wasteful the decision might have been—ultimately contributed, in some small degree, to the benefit of society as a whole. And if enough people acted similarly, the resulting benefits would be replicated multi-fold, resulting in an overall net positive impact on the world.

So men: the next time you find yourself teetering back-and-forth when trying to decide whether or not to purchase those overpriced-yet-desirable Michelin PAX tires for the over-priced-yet desirable sports car you purchased, say "What the f**k," and go for it. Because, in the end, that $36,000 tire purchase will ultimately have a positive impact on you, your loved ones, and the world.

And ladies, my advice to you is simple: Buy the shoes and eat the chocolate!

CHAPTER

THE JOYFUL RELIEF OF HAPPINESS

02

When I purchased that $5,000 suit, the purchase made me happy. Like me, I am sure that, at some point in your life, you have experienced something, done something, or had something done to you that has made you happy. But what exactly do we mean when we say that we are "happy"? Got a good grade on a test? "I'm happy!" Met a new guy who has a job, doesn't live in his parents' basement, and likes cats? "Oh, you make me so happy!" Your team won the game? "You can't believe how happy I am!" It's Friday at 5PM? "I'm happy the weekend is finally here!" Got your period this month? "Whew! I never thought I'd be happy to see *that*!" But what do you really *mean*? How do you describe what you are feeling when you say that you are "happy"? In a way, happiness is like being in love: you can't exactly explain what it is or what it feels like, but you know it when you experience it.

Every day we encounter people who exclaim to the world that they are "so happy!" But when you ask those people to describe what it feels like to be "so happy," they can't. Some people will say that it feels *good*, and others might say that it's like a big party going on inside their body. But in the end, everyone will struggle when trying to put their feelings of "happiness" into words — it's an emotion experienced by millions of people each and every day that no one can describe.

If you are like most of these millions of people, you have probably never given a moment's thought to describing what it feels like to be "happy." Why don't you give it a shot? Tough, isn't it? And to make matters worse, happiness is not a universal; some people's happiness is *joyful* ("I'm engaged!") and some people's happiness is simply *relief* ("Thank god no one was injured in that car crash!"). For example, when couples have their first child you often hear them say "This is the happiest day of my life!" And if you were to ask them what that feels like, they might say something like "I am just overjoyed!" or "Words just can't explain it" (my point exactly). But however the couple answers the question, their description would be a "joyful" one. And what about the person who has been accused of murder? Facing life in prison if convicted, he hears the jury read their verdict: "We, the jury, find the defendant ... not guilty." It is very likely that this person would also describe that day as being the happiest day of his or her life. However, if you asked that person to describe what it felt like, they would probably say "Relief!"

There is a big difference between a feeling of *joy* and a feeling of *relief*. Yet, it would be hard to argue that both the new parents and the accused murderer are not extremely happy and experiencing the happiest day of their lives. So what does that say about happiness—other than that everyone who experiences it cannot completely explain what it feels like? And if people cannot describe what it feels like to be happy, then is it possible to know what it takes for someone to be happy? Is happiness a short-term feeling ("I'm having a good day today") or a long-term state of being ("I am always happy")? Is it possible to be permanently happy ("I have a happy life")?

When I purchased that over-priced $5,000 suit and walked out of the store with it, I was very happy. One week later, my feelings about the suit purchase were no longer happy, but neutral. And by the time I received my credit card bill in the mail a few weeks later showing a charge of $5,495 for a *suit*, any lingering feelings of happiness I had were replaced with feelings of *bleh*! In my case, the feeling of happiness I received from the purchase of the suit was short-term. Sure, I am still grateful that I own the suit, but I can't say that owning it still makes me "happy."

But what does that *mean*? I believe that happiness is like the common cold. A "cold" is more than just one thing; it's a combination of things—symptoms—including fatigue, stuffy nose, coughing, sneezing, sore throat, runny nose, earache, stiff neck, and a fever. Some or all of these factors may or may not be present when the subject says that he or she has a "cold."

People often define happiness by what prompts it: material prosperity; emotional well-being, physical pleasure, or personal flourishing. Happiness is important enough to the human psyche that a specialty is now devoted entirely to its research. This area of study is called positive psychology.

Positive psychology is the scientific study of "the strengths and virtues that enable individuals and communities to thrive." This field studies positive emotions and happiness, which is just as important to understanding human psychology as mental illness is. Understanding what makes people happy can enable clinicians to develop ways to help people recover from certain experiences and possibly help prevent specific disorders.

While happiness may be subjective from one individual to the next, researchers have still been able to measure it scientifically because people are able to report on the state of their happiness and judge its increases and decreases. Psychologist Daniel Gilbert says it's akin to how optometrists are able to measure eyesight: the only way to come up with a prescription is by asking patients "is it clearer like this…or like this?"

Psychologists concentrate on three primary sources of happiness: *heredity*, which encompasses temperament and personality; *life circumstances*, including prosperity and health; and an individual's *personal life choices*. Generally speaking, people overestimate the importance of life circumstances when it comes to happiness. How often have you heard someone say, or have you felt yourself, "if I just had more money", "if I had a better job", "if only I could find my soul mate", or "I wish I woulda left that bastard a long time ago...then I'd be happy, or at least happier"?

People as a whole tend to put the responsibility for their happiness on external factors, but many positive psychologists have found that people have a lot more control over their happiness than they know, or perhaps want to believe. Research by psychologist Sonja Lyubomirsky suggests half of our happiness is genetic. Some people are literally just born happier than others. Just ten percent of our happiness is beyond our control, and forty percent of our happiness is controlled by our own choices and actions. So, unless you are simply *born* a miserable sonofabitch, this research suggests that we are responsible for our own happiness and that happiness is based on the choices we make. So, in order to give ourselves the best chance at being happy, we should do the things we want to do based on our self-interest.

Understanding how much control we have over our emotional destiny enables people to feel less a victim of fate and more like the master of it. Research suggests that cultivating positive emotions is a significant way to be happier. Such emotions include gratitude, serenity, hope, pride, and love.

Research by Martin Seligman (considered the founder of positive psychology) found a paradox: removing unhappiness from someone does not leave them happy; it leaves them empty. This finding had a direct impact on treatment, which traditionally was all about removing unhappiness. It was also what prompted him to develop positive psychology as a field.

In his book *Flourish: A Visionary New Understanding of Happiness and Well-being*, Seligman argues that genuine well-being comes from promoting five elements of well-being: pleasure, engagement, relationships, meaning, achievement—also known as P.E.R.M.A. *Pleasure* is, simply put, feeling good. *Engagement* is associated with having a good, full life comprised of satisfying work, close relationships with family and friends, and interesting hobbies. *Meaning* refers to feeling part of a larger purpose. *Meaning* and *achievement* are consistent with Maslow's need for *self-actualization*. While all the elements of well-being are important, they are not equally important. Seligman believes *engagement* and *meaning* are most crucial for having a happy life; two elements that are directly determined by people acting in their own self-interest.

That said, every person is different so there is no one definitive path to happiness for everyone. It seems that it's not as important that we *achieve* happiness as long as we seek out the elements that might enable happiness to happen. The more individuals nurture these elements, Seligman believes, the more fulfilled their lives will be and the happier they will ultimately be. In other words, the more we take control of our lives and do the things that we want to do for our own self-interested reasons, the happier we will become.

Not all happiness is the same, posits psychologist Daniel Kahneman. Kahneman differentiates between the *experiencing self* and the *remembering self*, which separates the moment-by-moment feelings of happiness prompted by positive emotions from descriptions of experiences produced when recalling or remembering these experiences. Kahneman believes happiness is basically a juggling act between these two types of happiness.

Experienced happiness depends primarily on personality and on the activities people choose to spend their time on. Because we have the ability to act in our self-interest and determine which activities we spend our time on, we can dictate our own experienced happiness to a great degree.

Perhaps the most important aspect of happiness is how it tangibly benefits people. Studies by Psychologist Ed Diener, one of the most well-respected researchers in the field of positive psychology, found compelling evidence that happiness improves physical health and lengthens lives. So much so that some research suggests overall health and well-being can be significantly impacted by simply being happy. And since people can dictate their own happiness by acting in their self-interest, people, therefore, have the ability to affect their health and well-being through their actions.

Is it possible to be permanently happy or is happiness only a short-term, fleeting emotion? Unless you are imbrued with major affective disorder, pleasant type (a psychiatric disorder of happiness), I don't believe it is possible to be permanently happy. I say this because there will always be something that comes along to interrupt one's happiness. Your wedding day's the happiest day of your life? The post-honeymoon reality of living together will interrupt that. You're happy because you got an 'A' in gym class? The realization that you have a calculus exam tomorrow will cut that happiness short. You're happy with the purchase of your spanking-new Porsche automobile? Your first car insurance payment will bring you back down to earth.

Happiness is situational, and therefore, most of our happiness is short-term. Long-term happiness results from either the memories we have of our short-term happy experiences (e.g. the birth of your first child) or from the increased frequency of happy experiences. For example, if you are happy or have happy experiences for 300 days of the year, then you can be considered to have had a happy year. If you are 30 years old and you have had 25 such happy years, then you can be considered to have lived a relatively happy life. This, of course, assumes that the magnitude of the happiness-interrupters (such as a tragic event, for example) are not so severe as to overwhelm the otherwise happy events you've experienced. We can dictate our ability to have more happy (positive) experiences than negative, unhappy ones by making the decision to engage in those activities and seek those experiences that *we* determine will bring us pleasure, satisfy a need, and make us feel happy.

The Spread of Happiness

Harvard University social scientist Dr. Nicholas Christakis and University of California at San Diego Political Science professor James Fowler reported the findings of a 20-year study that showed how emotions can pass from person-to-person up to three degrees of separation away. The findings suggest that a person's happiness may be determined by how happy the person's friends' friends' friends are, even if some of the friends' friends are total strangers to the person. Christakis states that, in terms of happiness, everyday interactions we have with other people are contagious.

If a person's happiness can spread to others, then it stands to reason that the effects of happiness—such as health improvement benefits and pro-social behaviors—are multiplied every time a person is happy, increasing the overall health and productivity of a group or society.

The Spread of Happiness

One person's happiness can spread to as many as 39 other people

Spreads

Benefits

CHAPTER

"WHY DID I BUY THAT SUIT!?

03

On that occasional lazy Sunday morning when I am bored senseless with absolutely nothing to do, my mind will tend to wander and, when it does, I ponder such insignificant questions as: Since the word *mile* is derived from the Latin word for 1,000, then why is a mile 5,280 feet and not just 1,000 feet? Or: Why does the National Football League use *Super Bowl XLVII* in Roman numerals instead of simply calling it *Super Bowl 47*? And, a while back, I even asked myself: Why did I spend $5,000 on a *suit*? On the surface, this last question might seem like an easy one to answer: Because the purchase made me *feel good*. But *why* did I buy the suit? Buying the suit because it made me feel good is a superficial, or *extrinsic* reason. But what is the deeper, internal, *intrinsic* reason why I purchased the suit? Is there some need buried deep down inside me that screamed out, "For your very existence, you need to buy that suit!"? What exists within us humans that compels us to do the things that we do?

Have you ever had such contemplative moments? Have you ever really sat down and thought about *why* you did something? Sure, there are lots of reasons why we do things, but have you ever thought about the *real* reason behind why you did something—not at the surface or extrinsic level, but at the fundamental or intrinsic level? What motivated you to take the action that you took? As a child, for instance, when your parents told you to "Put down that knife," you did so because they *told* you to. You learned at an early age that it was in your best interest to do what they told you to do as a means of avoiding the sting of a belt or a switch. (Speaking of which, do people still beat their children with *switches*? Come to think of it, do people even spank their children *at all* anymore? If not, then I grew up in the wrong era).

But I digress.

In this case, at the surface, the reason you put down the knife was because your parents told you to do so. This is an example of your behavior and actions being driven by the expectation of a reward or punishment depending on the way you responded to your parents' instruction. If you put down the knife as instructed, you were likely to receive some type of reward such as a pleasant "Thank you," a kind pat on the head, a piece of candy or—the latest in a ridiculous series of twenty-first century suburban ideas—*points*. (Don't get me started). Such positive reinforcement ultimately led you to develop a routine behavior of following your parents' instructions and a lovely, obedient child you became. On the other hand, if you'd refused to follow your parents' instruction to put down the knife, your behavior would likely have been followed by a negative consequence such as a verbal scolding, a spank on the butt, or … five lashes from a *switch*! The negative reinforcement or punishment would eventually have conditioned you to obey your parent's instruction if, for no other reason, than to avoid your parents' wrath.

Both of these methods of conditioning—offering positive rewards for being obedient and administering deterrent punishment for being disobedient—are *extrinsic* influences: non-essential external factors that influence our behavior, such as school grades, work evaluations, and other peoples' opinions of us.

Here's another scenario: you wake up on a Monday morning and get dressed to go to work. On this particular Monday you have to attend a four-hour meeting in the stuffy office conference room with the uncomfortable chairs. On days like this, you usually make it a point to wear your well-worn, pea-green, Fred G. Sanford hand-me-down sweater that you inherited from your older sibling several years ago, and your super comfortable Milly zip-pocket leather mini skirt. The reason you like wearing this sweater and skirt during long meetings in the stuffy conference room is because they are so comfortable and you never have to worry about spilling coffee on the sweater; coffee that will be much needed to make it through the four-hour meeting.

You look into your closet and are faced with a decision: do you wear the ugly pea-green sweater or do you wear your blue Brooks Brothers "professional" blouse that happens to be about as comfortable as wearing a plastic trash bag? After thinking about it for a short while and considering that your new boss will be attending the meeting, you decide to wear the blue professional blouse. Why? If the ugly sweater is what you really wanted to wear and the Brooks Brothers blouse is unbearably uncomfortable, why choose the blue blouse?

At the surface, you may have chosen the blue blouse because it matched your leather mini skirt. Or you may have chosen it because it complements the color of your eyes ... or your shoes ... or your purse. But most likely, you chose the blue blouse because you wanted to appear professional to your new boss and not have her think that you are some ugly-sweater-wearing, mini-skirt-sporting insubordinate who is probably not very smart. And if this is the reason, then your decision was based on external or extrinsic factors such as the opinion you fear your new boss might form about you and the impact that opinion could have on your work performance review. So, on one hand, you will make a positive first impression on your new boss by wearing the blue blouse—and a long, uncomfortable, dowdy skirt to go with it—but on the other hand, you will be uncomfortable and miserable for the four hours you have to sit in the stuffy conference room. This is an example of how we suppress our true desires in order to conform to other people's definitions of how we should act or what we should do.

American psychologist Edward Thorndike developed a concept that he called "The Law of Effect," which basically states that when people are rewarded for a certain behavior (e.g. the child being rewarded with a piece of candy for following the parents' instruction to put down the knife) they are likely to repeat that behavior more frequently. And when a person is punished for engaging in a certain behavior (e.g. receiving five lashes with a switch for not following the parents' instruction to put down the knife) that behavior is likely to occur less frequently. There is the possibility that people only engage in those activities, either positive or negative, that offer some type of personal reward or payoff. In other words, the personal payoff is what motivates people to do certain things and behave in certain ways.

If this idea of the personal payoff was applied to the examples of the child with the knife and the worker who decided to wear the blue shirt, we would find that: (a) the only reason why the child obeyed the parents' instruction and put down the knife was because the child knew that he or she would be rewarded with a piece of candy, or would be spared the pain of the switch; and (b) the only reason why the worker decided to wear the blue Brooks Brothers blouse to the meeting was because she believed that the new boss would view her more favorably if she wore the professional blouse rather than the ugly, pea-green sweater.

I agree that such extrinsic rewards and influences can modify and even shape behavior, but what are the long-term implications regarding behavior modification? Do the behaviors last or continue when there is no longer the inducement of an extrinsic reward or payoff? Would a person continue to engage in a certain behavior (such as wearing the uncomfortable blue Brooks Brothers blouse to the four-hour meeting or following their parents' instruction) when the person no longer *has* to? The answer is "yes" and "no."

Robots and Rebels: Why We Do Things

Arthur "The Fonz" Fonzarelli was a rebel. James Dean was a rebel. Madonna is a rebel. Steve McQueen was a rebel. Frank Serpico (the New York Police Department police officer who took a stand against corruption in the force) was a rebel. Malcolm X was a rebel. They are not "rebels" in the *Pancho Villa* sense—people who fight militaristic revolutionary or civil wars—but instead, are people who repudiated conformity, abhorred obedience, and were willing to go against mainstream opinion in the name of their principles. A rebel forms his or her *own* opinions—despite what others may think of them for doing so—and is someone who makes their own independent decisions about things that impact their lives. Rebels do things because they *want to*, not because they are *expected to*.

"Robots", on the other hand, are people who do things because they are instructed or conditioned to. They conform to the sentiment of the day and feel uncomfortable doing things that might incur unfavorable opinions from others. They are driven and motivated by reward, fear, and what other people think. The difference between a robot and a rebel is clear: When, for example, a police officer asks a robot why she parked her car in a restricted space, the robot would tell the officer that she is so sorry and that she will move her car right away. But when the police officer asks the rebel why she parked her car in a restricted space, the rebel would reply, "Because I *wanted* to."

The rebel's behavior can be described as being *autonomous*: they do things of their own volition and because they genuinely *want* to do them. They feel free to act in the manner which they decide, and when they make a decision, they embrace it with a sense of commitment. They do things because they have a genuine intrinsic (as opposed to extrinsic, or external) need to do it. In contrast, the robot's behavior can be described as *controlled*: they do things because they are instructed or pressured into doing them. Their actions and behaviors are not the result of their own intrinsic desire to do them, but because some external pressures are being exerted on them, compelling them to engage in a certain activity or behave a certain way. When controlled, people act without a sense of personal commitment. And when a person's behaviors are not self-determined or self-motivated, they function sub-optimally, become disassociated, unfulfilled, and even undervalued.

When a 12-year-old boy decides to climb a tree because he made the decision to do so for the fun of it, he will derive more fun and pleasure from the activity than the 12-year-old boy who climbs the tree to prove to his competitive father that he can. This illustrates how a person acting autonomously will embrace and genuinely enjoy an activity to a greater degree because he made the decision to do it for himself, not because he was compelled to do it. In this example, the 12-year-old boy who acted autonomously and decided to climb the tree based on his intrinsic motivation to engage in an activity that interests him and not due to some external compulsion (a father's expectations) can be said to have acted in a self-determined manner.

Self-Determination is a person's ability to freely choose the acts in which he or she engages without the intrusion of external interference. Research has shown that when our decisions are self-determined, we begin to satisfy our basic psychological needs for autonomy, relevance, and affiliation, among others. To the extent that these needs are continually satisfied determines how well people develop, function effectively and experience wellness. This is why it is important for people to act of their own free will. Because, in the end, people are motivated to fulfill basic needs and therefore, all human behavior is aimed toward the satisfaction of these basic human needs. And until our needs are satisfied, we can never be fulfilled.

When I purchased that suit, my decision was based

on my own self-determination and I made the decision autonomously. But—as the proposition I offered in the preceding paragraph suggests—that implies that I purchased the suit to satisfy or fulfill some intrinsic, fundamental human need and not just because the purchase made me feel good. So what basic need could I have been trying to satisfy by purchasing and spending too much money on a suit? What basic need could the worker have been trying to satisfy by wearing the blue Brooks Brothers blouse instead of her preferred Fred G. Sanford pea-green sweater?

Needs as Motivation

In his 1943 paper, *A Theory of Human Motivation*, and his later book, *Motivation and Personality*, psychologist Abraham Maslow proposed that all human behavior is motivated by need; specifically, a hierarchy of needs. He referred to it as a hierarchy—often depicted as a pyramid—because our primary, basic needs (such as food or shelter) must be satisfied before we can move on to satisfy higher-level needs, such as the need for companionship. Maslow believed that needs create instinctual behaviors in people which motivate us to behave in ways that satisfy those needs.

According to Maslow, the appearance of one need is contingent upon the prior satisfaction of another, lower-level need. These basic physiological needs are considered a greater priority than higher needs on the pyramid. They must be met before the person can move up the hierarchy. In other words, a person who is starving will not be concentrating on building his self-esteem.

Maslow's original theory consisted of five needs. The first are physical needs; the instinctive basic needs necessary for survival, which include food, water, oxygen, and sleep. Until these needs are met, all other needs are secondary. Once the basic needs are met, man can turn his attention to safety and security. To early man, that would have been a cave and a fire to keep away predators. To modern man, it refers to employment, shelter, medical care, and a safe environment in which to live. The next level up in the hierarchy encompasses social, or emotional, needs such as friendship, a sense of belonging, romantic love, and general affection. If we can't find companionship in other people, we'll seek it out in community groups, religions, and even our pets. Once we are secure in our survival needs, safety and personal relationships, self-esteem becomes important. This manifests as a desire for external recognition and individual accomplishment. We don't need it to survive, but we do need it to feel good about ourselves.

This need for esteem leads directly to the top of the pyramid: self-actualization. This is when an individual focuses on personal growth and is less concerned about other people's opinions. The goal is to reach and fulfill their potential. Maslow defined self-actualization as the process of personal developing in order to achieve and maximize one's potential.

Maslow deemed the first four levels as deficiency needs, or D-needs, because they are caused by some type of deprivation. He labeled self-actualization as a being need, or B-needs, because it wasn't prompted by a lack of something but by a desire to grow as a person. Self-actualization is person-specific. Maslow points out that, for one person, it could be a desire to be an outstanding parent; for another, it could be to express oneself through the arts or in science.

Behavior conducive to self-actualization involves trying new things and engaging in new experiences; going outside the envelope; avoiding pretense; and taking responsibility. The benefits of self-actualization include a deeper appreciation of the world, more loving relationships, increased compassion and a heightened support of others.

Critics of Maslow say it is difficult, if not impossible, to quantitatively test his theory of self-actualization, which makes it difficult to test scientifically. Perhaps. But his primary legacy was to introduce a new perspective and paradigm: focusing on healthy psychological development supported by taking control of one's own life and acting toward the satisfaction of needs.

It could be extremely challenging (and possibly useless?) to develop a comprehensive list of fundamental human needs because the number of needs one can think of could be infinite, depending on the level of specificity used to describe the need. That said, as a reference, I have provided an interpretation of the human needs as Maslow identified them.

AN INTERPRETATION OF MASLOW'S HIERARCHY OF NEEDS

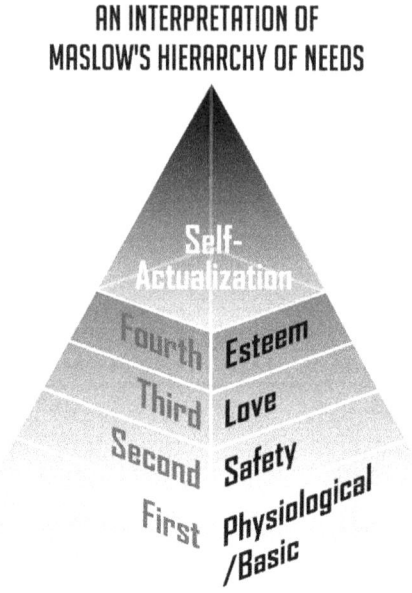

Types of Needs

The Physiological Needs	Examples
The basic needs, or physiological drives, that are considered the starting point for motivation. Until these needs are satisfied, human beings cannot function optimally (if at all).	Food Shelter Water Sleep Oxygen

The Safety Needs	Examples
People have a need to feel safe and free from danger and harm. We have a desire to live in an orderly, predictable, organized world in which unexpected, unmanageable, or dangerous things do not take place. And, if they happen to, we have the ability to protect ourselves.	Security Stability Order Physical Safety

The Love Needs	Examples
If both the physiological and the safety needs are fairly well-gratified, then the needs for love, affection and a sense of belonging will emerge. A person will noticeably feel the absence of friends, or a partner, or a spouse, or children. She will hunger for affectionate relations with people in general, namely, for a place in a group, and she will strive with great intensity to achieve this goal. The person will want to attain such a position more than anything else in the world and may even forget that once, when she was hungry, she didn't give love and affection the slightest thought.	Affection Identification Companionship

The Esteem Needs	Examples
Satisfaction of the self-esteem need leads to feelings of self-confidence, worth, strength, adequacy, and the capability to be useful and necessary in the world. But the thwarting of these needs produces feelings of inferiority, weakness, and helplessness.	Self-respect Prestige Success Respect of others

The Need for Self-Actualization	Examples
Even if all these other needs are satisfied, we may still often (if not always) expect that a new discontent and restlessness will soon develop, unless the individual is doing what he or she was meant to do. If they are to be ultimately happy, a musician must make music, an artist must paint, a poet must write. What a man can be, he must be. This need is called self-actualization.	Self-fulfillment Understanding Achieving one's own potential

A study published in 2011 by a University of Illinois researcher found that fulfillment of Maslow's identified needs was strongly related to happiness. This implies that a person can achieve happiness by satisfying his or her needs, and the best way that a person can contribute to the satisfaction of his or her needs is by doing the things that *they determine* will bring this satisfaction about; in other words, acting in their self-interest.

CHAPTER 04

THE GOODNESS OF SELF-INTEREST

SELFLESSNESS

At this point, it is worth discussing the difference between being "selfish" and acting in one's "self-interest"; there is a difference. In this context, it is also worthwhile to discuss the idea of being "self-less." Some people believe that to be *self-less* is noble and is the opposite of being *selfish* or even *self-interested*. I disagree, primarily because I don't believe that, if one is rational, it is possible to be truly *selfless*.

To be selfless is to have little or no concern for oneself. Is that likely? Is it even possible? Can a sane, rational person walk out into highway traffic and have little or no concern for his or her physical well-being? Is it conceivable that a billionaire (who has to be somewhat sane in order to accrue all that money) would give all of her wealth, her house, her cars, and all of her possessions to the needy and then go live in a refrigerator box on Skid Row? I believe not. Hell, even Buddhist monks who renounce all worldly possessions and earthly pleasures still maintain self-concern. And if they did not, then I would argue that they are either insane or irrational.

And what about the belief favored by many—including Maslow, Thorndike and others—that people's actions are motivated by a desire to satisfy a need or to receive some sort of reward or payoff? You shoveled your neighbor's driveway? You want your neighbor to think highly of you. You helped an elderly woman across the street? You want to convince yourself or other people that you are a swell guy. You gave money to charity or tithe to the church? You want to feel good about yourself (a reward) or you are trying to score brownie points with your deity. You offered to help the attractive woman put her luggage in the airplane's overhead storage compartment? You want her to like you and you are hoping that you can convince her to go on a date with you. The proof? You let the unattractive woman struggle to store *her* luggage all by herself.

If these theories are to be believed, then the person who is supposedly acting selflessly would be doing so based on some self-interest (to satisfy a need, to receive some reward, to make themselves happy). If so, that person would still not be acting without regard for self (selflessly).

I think that many people confuse being selfless with being altruistic, philanthropic, benevolent, or some other such affiliative behavior through which people show compassion and a sense of cooperation toward the performance and survival of humanity. In other words, they are simply being neighborly. And just like those people who believe their actions are selfless, when people act altruistically they are, at least subconsciously, doing so with the expectation of receiving some form of payoff for their behavior. When actress Sally Struthers appealed to your sense of charity and motivated you to give $0.70 cents per day to the Christian Children's Fund (ChildFund) so that you could feed the little African boy, Jamal, did you do so selflessly? No. Did you do it because you wanted to see Jamal grow up to be a healthy, productive person? No. You did it for the same reason you spend $0.70 cents per day on coffee: It made you feel good, and that good feeling was not selfless; it was a reward and a payoff for your $0.70 cents contribution.

I believe that selflessness is not possible in the rational world because, by its very definition, it requires a person to give of himself and to have no regard for his own well-being. And a person who has no regard for himself or his well-being is indifferent about whether he lives or dies, which could lead the person to engage in irrational and possibly even self-destructive behaviors.

There is a children's book called *The Giving Tree* by Shel Silverstein about the relationship between a little boy and his tree. Every day the boy would go to the tree to eat its apples, swing from its branches, climb up and slide down its trunk; this made the tree happy and, as a result, the tree loved the boy. One day the boy went to the tree for some money, but the tree had no money. Instead, the tree told the boy that he could sell the tree's apples to earn some money. Then, the boy needed wood, so the tree said that the boy could cut off its branches and cut its trunk to have the wood; anything so that the boy would be happy. The boy used the wood to make a boat and sailed away. The tree had given of itself selflessly to ensure that the boy was happy. And, in the end, the tree had nothing left to give anyone else; it was just an unhappy stump.

This simple story illustrates another problem with the idea of genuine selflessness: Research has shown that intense selflessness can be associated with a variety of disorders, and that to be truly and totally selfless is to be self-destructive. This can materialize, for example, as anorexia or sometimes as tolerance of abusive relationships. Those in relationships such as these often believe that, with enough self-sacrifice (selflessness), they can persuade their batterers to reform.

According to Dr. Rachel Bachner-Melman, a clinical psychologist at Hadassah University Medical Center in Jerusalem who specializes in eating disorders, young women who act extremely selflessly are so sensitive to the needs of others that they deny their own needs and barely feel they have the right to exist. And they apologize for themselves by ceaselessly giving.

Is that degree of selflessness rational? I believe it is not and, as I stated previously, I do not believe that it is possible for a rational person to be genuinely selfless. Not long ago, I had a conversation on this topic with a friend of mine who argued: "Bobby Brown!? Bobby Brown!? Now THAT is some selfless sh*t!" My friend was referring to an incident that was described by R&B singer Bobby Brown, and former husband of singer Whitney Houston, on his 2005 Bravo reality television show "Being Bobby Brown." In this episode, Bobby described how one evening an acquaintance was complaining that she was constipated. So in order to help her out, Bobby went into the bathroom and used his hand to facilitate the process. This, my friend argued, was an act of pure selflessness. Call it what you want, but to me, that was just plain *nasty*!

Selfishness vs. Self-Interest: Is There a Difference?

Two terms that are often interchanged and misconstrued are "selfish" and "self-interest." Contrary to what you may have learned, the two words have completely different meanings. While the array of dictionaries and academic articles offer various definitions for the two words—some even going so far as to define selfishness as being self-interested—I will provide you with my take on the differences:

To be selfish is to be concerned almost exclusively with oneself and one's own advantage, pleasure, or well-being—and this is the key point: *without regard for other people*. Selfish-acting people inconsiderately engage in selfish behavior; the only thing that matters to the selfish person is their own payoff—everyone and everything else be damned! If the selfish-acting peanut butter sandwich lover wants to have a sandwich but doesn't want to eat alone, he will coerce his peanut-allergic girlfriend into eating a peanut butter sandwich, too, just so that he can have some company. And the likelihood that the peanut butter sandwich lover's innocent girlfriend will become sick as a result of his coercion? Too bad.

Selfish people cultivate the concept of egocentrism, believing that the world revolves around them and is there simply to serve their interests and desires. If a selfish man wants to buy a pack of cigarettes but his wife needs the $5 to travel to and from her job—a job that she will lose if she is late for work—the selfish man's response would be: "Make that Marlboro Light, please."

There was an award-winning Broadway play by Lorraine Hansberry entitled *A Raisin in the Sun*, which became a major motion picture in 1961 starring actor Sidney Poitier. It is a story about a family living on the South Side of Chicago whose matriarch becomes the beneficiary of a $10,000 life insurance payment. The family is conflicted over how to use the money, money that will afford the family many options to get ahead in life. One of the family members, Walter Lee, wants to go into business with friends who plan to open a liquor store.

So, unbeknownst to the other family members, Walter Lee selfishly invests the money into the liquor store and eventually loses it all. Walter Lee acted selfishly because he invested the money in a risky business venture without regard for the interests of (or consequences for) the other members of his family.

The behavior of selfish individuals—whether the behavior is purposeful, accidental, or unconscious—is often detrimental to others, suggesting that, in order for selfishness to occur, other people must be involved. If Fred went to the bank and withdrew his family's entire life's savings just so he could light it on fire because he likes the smell of burning money, his actions would be considered selfish. However, if Fred was the last surviving person on earth and he went to the bank and withdrew his family's entire life's savings just to light it on fire because he likes the smell of burning money, would that be considered selfish? I say, no, because Fred's actions would have no impact on anyone else; there would be no negative consequences of his actions because no one would care. And if Fred's actions couldn't negatively impact other people or himself, then his actions would be considered *self-interested*; the difference is the involvement of other people.

One of the key differentiators between *selfishness* and *self-interest* is "sympathy." Philosopher Adam Smith, author of the classic works *The Theory of Moral Sentiments* and *An Inquiry into the Nature and Causes of the Wealth of Nations*, espoused this idea by suggesting that when being sympathetic, we attempt to identify with the feelings of others to the extent that our own sense of well-being depends to some degree on theirs and vice versa. He went on to write that "Sympathy cannot be regarded as a selfish principle," and no society can dismiss it without eventually suffering destructive consequences. The suggestion—one with which I agree—is that a (if not *the*) major difference between *selfishness* and *self-interest* is the idea that people acting in their own self-interest are, indeed, sympathetic to and considerate of others. So, while selfishness is being excessively concerned or obsessed with *yourself*, self-interest is being concerned for your own well-being, as well as the well-being of others.

Self-interest is integral to personal survival. It is in our self-interest to have food and shelter. It is in our self-interest to exercise and take care of our health. It is in our self-interest to have a job and earn enough money to support basic needs. Self-interest is an essential component of our overall sense of well-being. Self-interest—satisfying one's needs—*is not mutually exclusive from caring for others*.

Science 2.0 blogger Gerhard Adam makes an interesting point when he notes that self-interested behavior is behavior that you engage in at every moment. When you eat, you're behaving in a self-interested fashion; when you sleep, you're behaving in a self-interested manner. He argues that there is nothing that one can do that isn't self-interested. This idea would be consistent with those of Maslow and Thorndike who also believe that all human behavior is directed toward the satisfaction of a need (eating and sleeping) or in anticipation of a payoff or reward. This reward can be something as intangible as happiness or as tangible as monetary wealth.

In Chapter Two: *The Joyful Relief of Happiness*, I discussed how forty percent of our happiness is controlled by our own choices and actions. So, in order to give ourselves the best chance at being happy, we must make an effort to engage in those activities that serve our intrinsic self-interest, and are not based on external influences.

Psychologist Ed Diener offers one of the best descriptions of "happiness" that I have come across. He describes it as a combination of life satisfaction and *having more positive emotions than negative emotions*. And the way to experience more positive than negative emotions is to engage in those activities that will bring us pleasure, satisfy a need, and generally make us feel good. When we act in our self-interest, we seek out these feel-good activities and experiences that encourage happiness.

Self-Interest to Happiness

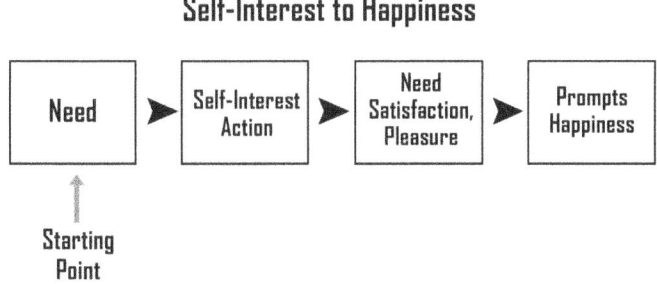

While acting in one's self-interest is about doing what one wants in order to achieve satisfaction and fulfillment, the impact these choices will have on others is always considered. If the self-interested decision-maker determines that her actions will significantly negatively impact others, she will reconsider engaging in the activity. This does not mean, however, that the self-interested decision-maker will not do anything that might have a negative impact on others; just that this factor will be taken into consideration. And if the decision-maker determines that the degree of the impact is not injurious or significant enough to dissuade her from engaging in the desired activity, she will go forward with the activity. This type of decision-making requires rational judgment so that the decision-maker can make an honest and realistic determination of the consequences of her actions. She can do this—per Adam Smith—by being sympathetic to those who may be impacted by her self-interested action. This sympathetic evaluation is often done subconsciously. For instance, when you drink a glass of water to quench your thirst, do you consciously think about the impact that drinking the water will have on others? Unless you and a friend are stranded in a desert, I would think not.

The table below is provided to help illustrate the subtle differences that can exist between that which is selfish and that which is self-interested.

THE GOODNESS OF SELF-INTEREST

An Example of "Selfish"	An Example of "Self-Interest"
When stranded in the sweltering heat of the desert with a friend, drinking the last remaining bottle of water all by yourself so that you can stay alive.	When stranded in the sweltering desert with a friend, drinking half of the water in the bottle so that you both can stay alive.
Working on an important project with a team of people and, when it's time to present the results of the project to an audience of important bigwigs, taking the stage alone and implying that you did all of the work by yourself.	Working on an important project with a team of people and, when it's time to present the results of the project to an audience of important bigwigs, sharing the stage with your teammates, stressing that it was a team effort, and making your contribution to the project sound valuable.
Men bathing themselves in awful-smelling, cheap cologne, rubbing it on their hands, and then shaking other people's hands leaving that overbearing smell on the other people's hands, too.	Applying only enough cologne to be smelled if someone is within your "personal zone": six inches from your body. And washing your hands afterward! You will still get the aromatherapy benefit of smelling your favorite fragrance throughout the day, but your use of the fragrance won't be excessive and off-putting to others.

An Example of "Selfish"	An Example of "Self-Interest"
Women wearing your Manolo Blahniks with the 5" heels while you are eight months pregnant so that you can still look fabulous.	Wearing your fabulous-yet-safer Manolo Blahnik Flat Blacks—understanding that, when pregnant, your weight increases, your body shape changes, and your center of gravity changes. These changes make you walk differently and less steadily, increasing your chances of falling and possibly hurting the baby and yourself.
Men: Arriving at your wife's company Christmas party wearing a pink Hello Kitty ballet tutu because you want to express yourself.	Arriving at your wife's Christmas party wearing slacks and a shirt, and saving the tutu for either when you get home or for YOUR company Christmas party. By doing this, you will still get the gratification and fulfillment of self-expression, but you will do so at your own professional expense and not your wife's.

Dale T. Miller, from the Department of Psychology at Princeton University, says that people's actions must, at least crudely, conform to the strictures of neoclassical economic theory. This is consistent with other theories of self-interested behavior which state that our actions are based on positive payoffs and rewards, whether that's the pleasure that comes from satisfying a need, making a profit in the stock market, or avoiding painful experiences.

The notion that humans are predominantly self-interested is central to many theories of human behavior, and the belief that self-interest dominates human affairs is also prominent in scientific theories. Research suggests that people rarely act in a manner that is incongruent with their self-interest. These studies support the idea that acting in our own self-interest is not only natural, but also necessary for societal development, personal fulfillment, and even survival of the species. For these reasons, people must be free to pursue courses of action that they determine are beneficial to them; people must be free to act *individualistically*.

At its most direct, *individualism* is based on a person's inherent legal right to pursue personal happiness. Free people are able to do whatever they want to do without the restriction of an oppressive or unjust government or dictator. And no society can be civilized without recognizing people's individual rights to do and act as they please toward their personal happiness; in other words, a group has no rights other than the individual rights of its members.

The United States was founded on this very ideal of individualism. In the Declaration of Independence, the country's founders stated: "We hold these truths to be self-evident, that all men are created equal, that they are endowed by their Creator with certain unalienable Rights, that among these are Life, Liberty and the pursuit of Happiness."

Dr. Shawn E. Klein of the Department of Philosophy at Rockford College argues that every significant innovation and advancement in America's history is a direct result of our country's willingness to embrace individualism. Klein points out that while individualism inherently presumes independence, initiative, and personal responsibility, it also requires cooperation with others to maintain the necessary balance so that each party is free to pursue their vision of happiness. This suggests that we can come together as individuals for common social, cultural, and political goals without losing individuality.

In *Democracy in America*, political philosopher Alexis de Tocqueville espouses a complex vision of American individualism because he saw it coexisting with a deep concern for friends and family, an enthusiasm for joining local community groups and professional organizations, and a commitment to a government of, by, and for the people. Tocqueville's take was that individualism is *not* synonymous with isolation or selfishness; instead, it is a way to further one's own goals and happiness by cooperating with other individuals as they pursue their goals. Believing that one can do as they please without regard for others is *not* individualism, it is *selfishness*, because individualism requires the acknowledgment that others have the same inalienable rights as one's self. This is a key distinction between self-interest and selfishness.

Unlike selfishness, self-interest is not a "zero-sum game": a situation in which one participant's gains result only from another participant's equivalent losses. In other words, where the net change in total gain among the participants is zero; the prize just shifts from one to the other. For example, if you have a dollar and I win your dollar from you in a game of cards, I will have $2 and you will be left with nothing. In this example, the number of dollars didn't change (we started with a total pot of $2), but my gain resulted in you being left with nothing: Zero.

This idea that self-interest is not a zero-sum game remains true when we interact with someone and we believe that person will pursue their own self-interest during our interaction (e.g. a business deal). We will pursue our own self-interest when we anticipate self-interested behavior from the person with whom we are interacting. This is due to our fear that, if we do not act in our self-interest in this situation, we might be exploited. And the more strongly we expect those with whom we are interacting to pursue a self-interested strategy, the more inclined we are to pursue a self-interested strategy ourselves, leading to competition. And that's a good thing because competition begets cooperation—which, by the way, is based on mutual self-interest.

Imagine a sporting event in which its competitors failed to adhere to the rules of the competition; neither the event nor the sport could thrive. It is in the financial best interest of the competitors to participate in a sport that is thriving, therefore, it is in their self-interest to cooperate with each other to ensure that the rules of the competition are adhered to and enforced. This notion of competition begetting cooperation also exists in the business community. Hewlett-Packard, Dell, and Apple are fierce technology competitors that would like nothing more than to beat each other into bankruptcy. Each of these technology behemoths relies on the Chinese component maker Foxconn to supply parts for their computer systems. Though H-P, Dell, and Apple are competitors, they all agree that it is in their companies' best interest to cooperate with each other to pressure Foxconn to enforce fair work conditions for its employees, for instance, and avoid a factory shut-down. If Foxconn became unable to supply computer components to H-P, Dell, and Apple, then all three of the technology companies would be negatively impacted.

Societies in which groups cooperate develop more quickly, have less conflict, and perform better, ultimately benefitting everyone in the cooperating groups. This was true of primitive societies where groups had to compete for limited resources or defend themselves against warring tribes. In these cases, cooperation would have allowed primitive man to coordinate their foraging behavior more efficiently, or form a more effective fighting unit to defend themselves and ensure their survival.

Some will argue that cooperation goes against naturalist Charles Darwin's theory of natural selection, which says that we should expect animals to behave in the way that best transmits their genes to future generations, thereby ensuring survival of the species. Therefore, cooperation is a potentially costly behavior that benefits other species. Nonetheless, examples of cooperation are pervasive throughout history, likely because in order to successfully overcome conflict and warfare between groups, the members of these groups need to cooperate.

In the same way that competition drives cooperation

as described in the scenarios above, so, too, does competition benefit societies through business enterprise. According to Chad Syverson, associate professor of economics at the University of Chicago and a productivity specialist, competition boosts productivity, helping companies to become more efficient and more viable. When they do, society benefits from more jobs, better goods and services, better infrastructure, better schools, and higher revenues, to name a few.

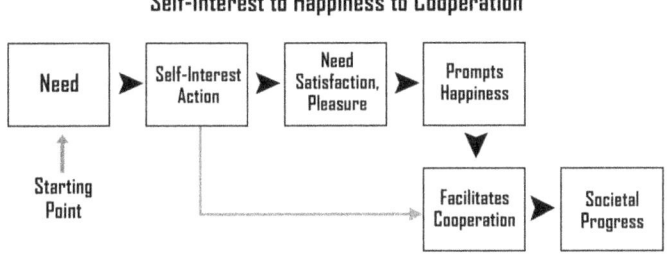

The Stigma of Self-Interest

Gerhard Adams made the point that sometimes people mistake self-interest for selfishness and end up feeling guilty for their personal and professional prosperity. This confusion between selfishness and self-interest appears to be widespread. In a 1991 American survey that was conducted to gauge people's perceptions of acting self-interested, eighty percent of respondents indicated that the tendency of people to look out only for their own interests was a serious problem in the United States; two-thirds of the respondents indicated that Americans were more concerned with their own activities and interests than with helping the needy; and almost two-thirds of respondents expressed the belief that people in our society were becoming less interested in helping one another. The problem with these responses is that people seemed to confuse "selfishness" with "self-interest." Either that or the respondents were not given a good understanding of the difference between the two.

It is important for people to understand the differences so that they stop feeling guilty about acting in their self-interest. Guilt is one of those negative emotions discussed earlier and, not only does it over-ride the positive emotions we're supposed to be feeling but it also keeps us from doing what we genuinely want to do. You may even have to play a Jedi mind trick on yourself and tell yourself that acting in your self-interest is NOT a bad thing. This reminds me of an encounter comedian Eddie Murphy described in his 1987 stand-up comedy film "Eddie Murphy Raw." In the film, Murphy describes a fictitious encounter with famous tough guy Mr. T, who was angry about some of the jokes Murphy had told about him.

Mr. T: "I heard you did some jokes about me."

Eddie Murphy: "No, you didn't."

Mr. T: "Maybe I didn't. I'm going to go beat up the fool that told me them lies."

THE GOODNESS OF SELF-INTEREST

If you have to use such an approach to re-program yourself into correctly believing that self-interest is not selfishness, and that acting in your self-interest is actually good, then, by all means, please do so.

Studies show that kids (and adults) develop into what you tell them they are because different expectations are placed on them based on how they are labeled. For example, a teacher who thinks that a student is smart may ask the student more challenging questions and praise the student more than the other students in the class. This added attention and praise may result in the student achieving better grades than their fellow students. This is known as a "self-fulfilling prophecy", the tendency for a person to foster certain behaviors that are consistent with the expectations applied to them. You will often hear this term used when referring to children who frequently misbehave. After a while, because they believe their parents *expect* them to behave badly, they continue to do so ("well, they think I'm going to screw up so I might as well").

If you think that acting in your self-interest carries the same stigma as selfishness, then you will act in a manner that avoids anything that could be construed as being selfish. If this is the case, you may never allow yourself the legitimately self-interested things you genuinely want, making yourself miserable. When people begin to embrace the idea that acting in our self-interest is a good thing, we will forge cooperative relationships with others who mutually act in *their* self-interest. And when this cooperation occurs, benefits result for all involved.

Lying

Any discussion about selfishness and self-interest warrants an examination of lying. Why? Because everyone lies or has at least told a lie at some point in their lives. And when we lie we either do so out of selfishness or our self-interest.

Is it ever in a person's self-interest to tell a lie, even if doing so does not negatively impact another person? To address this issue, it is necessary to define what it means to lie. Is a "little white lie" considered a significant lie or is it simply harmless speech? Is a "bold-faced lie" more egregious than a "little white lie"? Is "lying by omission" actually lying or is it a form of deception? And is deception lying? As these questions illustrate, there is a lot to consider when trying to determine whether or not lying is in a person's self-interest.

Lying can take many forms. In fact, some behaviors that one would never think of as deceptive—such as making a statement that is true at the moment the statement is made, but changes by the time someone investigates the statement's validity—are considered lying. For example, Jim the stock broker meets a young lady at a bar and tells the woman that he is a millionaire; a statement that is true at the moment that Jim shares this information with the woman. But overnight, there is a stock shift in the market and the value of Jim's stock plummets from $1.3 million to $25,000. When the woman learns that Jim is actually worth $25,000 and not $1.3 million, she will think that Jim lied to her in an attempt to impress her. In this example, some would believe that Jim told the woman a lie.

What some view as a misrepresentation of the truth, others will call a lie; what some might call *keeping a secret*, others will call a lie; what some might call *an honest mistake*, others will call a lie. When little Johnny wants to buy a $25 toy truck and his father—who doesn't have any money and therefore cannot afford to buy the truck—dishonestly tells Johnny that he can't have the truck because the paint used in that truck will make Johnny sick, would you consider that to be a lie of any significance? Or what about the poverty-stricken mother who tells little Betty that Betty cannot get that ice cream cone because it will rot little Betty's teeth—when, in fact, the real reason is because the mother simply cannot afford it and she doesn't want to discourage little Betty by telling her the truth about the family's unfortunate financial situation. Does that rise to the level of being a lie of any consequence? In both cases, I imagine most people would say no harm, no foul, and would characterize the parents' comments as harmless fibs. If so, then was it in the parents' self-interest to "fib" to their children? Many people would say that the parents were merely being deceitful, which raises the question: Is deception the same as lying?

To *deceive* is to mislead, usually through a false appearance or statement. To *lie* is to make a false statement with deliberate intent to deceive; it is an intentional untruth. While the definitions are similar, there is a subtle difference. The woman who puts on eye shadow, mascara, foundation, concealer, eyeliner, lipstick, and blush in order to enhance her looks is being deceitful—she is giving people the impression that her face is prettier than it actually is without make-up. But the woman who gets Botox (the drug that is injected into a person's face to remove the appearance of wrinkles in order to make the person look younger) prior to going to her school reunion—and tells her old classmates that she looks so young because she soaks her face in an ice bath every night—is lying. But even so, does it matter if it doesn't harm anyone or have any negative repercussions?

And what about that thing we all do when a total stranger or co-worker asks us a throw-away question like "Did you have a good weekend?" or "How are you this morning?" We say "Yes, it was good" to the former, and "I'm doing fine" to the latter, even if we had a shitty weekend and we feel awful that morning. Frankly, the questioner couldn't give a damn about how the answerer's feeling and the answerer doesn't give enough of a damn about the questioner's question to bother wasting any effort answering it. I call such answers to throw-away questions like these "resplying." To *resply* is to politely and harmlessly reply to an inconsequential question ("How are you this morning?") with a harmless lie ("I'm doing fine"). The father telling little Johnny that he can't have the truck because the paint will make him sick, and the mother telling little Betty that she can't have the ice cream cone because it will rot her teeth are both examples of *resplying*.

THE GOODNESS OF SELF-INTEREST

Resplying has a relationship with truthfulness. I believe that resplying is equivalent to making a statement that is mostly true. If a statement is mostly true then, by definition, it's not actually a lie, because the statement would be more true than false and—just like resplying—its impact would be largely inconsequential. When a coworker asks me "Did ya have a good weekend?" and I say "Yes, it was good"—even though my weekend sucked overall—my response simply means that it was mostly bad, but *some of it* was good. And since I'm not going to go into detail explaining my entire weekend to someone whom I consider undeserving of such an explanation, then I will resply. Cordially skipping the details is like an unwritten agreement between the questioner and the answerer: The questioner is asking the question to be polite and the answerer is throwing out a perfunctory answer to satisfy the questioner's expectation of a reply. For argument's sake, I will exclude the act of *resplying* from the category of *lying* in this discussion.

Why do people lie? Maslow would say that people lie to satisfy a need, and the type of need people attempt to satisfy by lying could vary. The lying person, for instance, could be attempting to satisfy a Safety need (job security, physical safety), a Love need (companionship), or an Esteem need (likeability, desirability, prestige, respect) through lying. However, lying to satisfy a lower-level need such as the need for companionship, for example, could negatively impact a higher-level need such as self-actualization. For this reason, it could be argued that lying is ultimately undesirable.

In his book, *Lying*, author Sam Harris argues that lying—even when it's about simple things— damages personal relationships and trust. He writes that most forms of vice and evil (such as adultery and corruption) are kindled and sustained by lies, and that we inflict unhappiness on ourselves by lying. If we accept his supposition as valid, then lies should be avoided if for no other reason than they make people unhappy. And anything that contributes to one's unhappiness is not in a person's self-interest.

Prosocial Behavior

Cooperation is a form of *prosocial behavior*. Prosocial behavior is voluntarily acting to help another person for no other extrinsic reason than to help. It is assistance offered without agenda or expectation. While it is tempting to equate prosocial behavior with altruism—which is selflessness to the point where a person is willing to sacrifice themselves for others—there are other factors that determine prosocial behavior. One of these factors is a person's mood. Research suggests that an individual who is happy or is in a good mood is more apt to help others than someone in a bad mood. It could be that when we're feeling good emotionally, we are more observant of others' needs, and when we are in a dark place, we are more focused on our own issues.

According to Adam Smith, empathy is a key differentiator between 'selfishness' and 'self-interest'. It is also a basis for prosocial behavior; we help because we can imagine being in the other person's position or can see the situation from their perspective.

Self-interested actions satisfy needs, provide people with pleasure, and make people happy. When people are happy, their mood is good. When people are in a good mood, they engage more frequently in prosocial behavior. Prosocial behaviors encourage reciprocity: if someone has helped you in the past you feel obligated to help them now. Or the opposite also applies: you help someone now with the unspoken belief that you will be helped, if needed, in the future. Prosocial behavior fosters cooperation and cooperation—as does mutual self-interest—helps societies thrive. Therefore, it can be argued that people acting in their mutual self-interest can have a positive impact on society, something often referred to as contributing to the Common Good.

The Common Good

The *common good* is a notion that originated over two thousand years ago and, since that time, an exact definition has proven to be elusive. In other words, a consensus regarding its true meaning has yet to be reached. Contemporary ethicist John Rawls defined the common good as "certain general conditions that are equally to everyone's advantage." A simpler definition of the common good is behavior that benefits one's society as a whole, whether that society is a family, an organization, a neighborhood, a nation, or mankind in general. To me, these two definitions provide the most effective descriptions of the concept of the common good.

The common good has also been used synonymously with "The Public Interest," in the sense that the common good is accessible to all members of society, and from which no one can be easily excluded. By this definition, the common good consists of the social systems, institutions, and environments on which we all depend, operating in a manner that benefits all people. Clean air, clean water, and public services can all be considered in the common good.

Back when hunter-gatherers formed small clans, self-interest and the common good were synonymous. But as nomadic tribes gave way to civilizations, human interaction within societies became much more complex and eventually self-interest and the common good existed on different planes. In modern times, the conflict between self-interest and common good is often set in economic terms. The Wall Street hedge fund brokers who made billions while millions of middle-class families lost their homes are the poster children for self-interest run amok at the expense of the common good. While these executives ostensibly worked in a service industry, one which was intended to benefit their clients, their behavior clearly encroached on selfishness.

But self-interest and financial success are not incompatible with the common good. For example, holding down a job is in an individual's self-interest, as are the creature comforts they buy with their earnings. That kind of consumer-driven spending—driven by the worker's self-interested decision to purchase items—improves the economy, which positively impacts the common good. Adam Smith wrote that "It is not from the benevolence of the butcher, the brewer, or the baker, that we expect our dinner, but from their regard to their own self-interest." Although the butcher established his butcher shop based on a self-interested decision to make profits—affording him the opportunity to live comfortably and more happily—his decision to do so benefits his community and therefore society by serving as a source of food for the shop's patrons and a source of additional tax revenue to the community. Ultimately, the butcher's self-interested decision to open the shop contributes to the common good of his neighborhood and society.

But as earlier stated, there has been no general agreement on a perfect definition of the common good. Novelist and philosopher Ayn Rand refutes the very notion of a common good, arguing that it is an undefinable concept. She wrote that there is no such living entity as "the public" (or "society," for that matter) but just a collection of individual people. Rand argues that when "the common good" of a society is regarded as something other than the individual good of its members, the good of some men will inevitably take precedence over the good of others. Therefore, says Rand, "the common good" means "the good of the majority," which is counter to the definition provided above whereby the common good should benefit *all* people.

I can appreciate Rand's position on the common good: nothing is good for everybody. Even in the case of clean air, there are certainly some factories —and therefore their employees—that have been negatively impacted as a result of clean air legislation. That said, we can all agree that having clean air and clean water is preferable by everyone, even those factory workers who might have lost their jobs because of it. Here's another way to think of it: Jane has some wood, Bill has some tools, Ann is an architect, and Butch is a craftsman. The four people bring their collective resources together and cooperate to build a house that they can all live in as shelter from the winter's cold. In this example, the house is the common good that resulted from their cooperation. And even though some trees were chopped down (ultimately harming animals and people) in order for Jane to procure the wood needed to build the house, they would all agree that it is in their best interest to have the house. Yes, the common good often requires trade-offs in other areas, but all who benefit from the common good will accept these trade-offs as necessary and justified.

Establishing and maintaining the common good requires the cooperation and cooperative efforts of people—the operative word being *cooperation*, an effort driven by the mutual *self-interest* of people. And since, by definition, the common good positively impacts most if not all members of society, there is a strong element of self-interest involved in contributing to the common good.

THE GOODNESS OF SELF-INTEREST

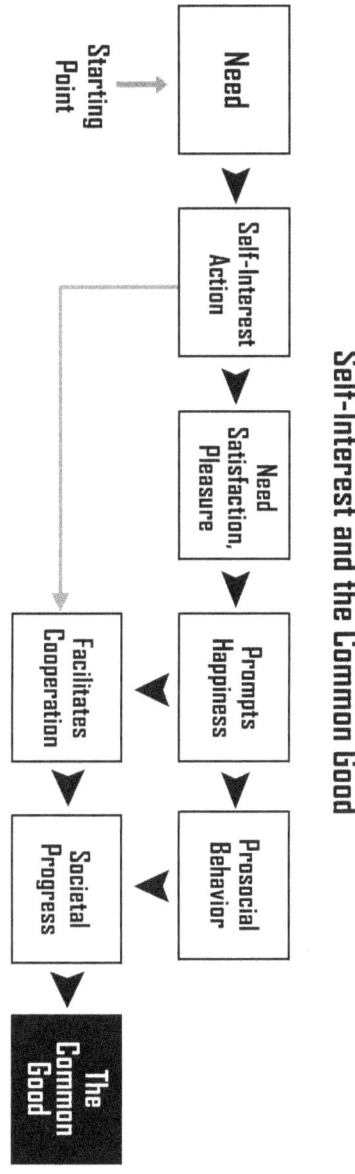

CHAPTER 05
"DAMN, I'VE GOTTA PEE"

"Of all the jive joints in the world she had to bring her big butt into mine!"

In the 1990s sketch comedy television show "In Living Color," actor-comedian Keenen Ivory Wayans (as Billy Dee Williams as Humphrey Bogart) offered his take on the classic 1943 movie "Casablanca" during a skit entitled "Ted Turner's Colorized Classics." In the skit, Keenen/Billy Dee/Bogart contemplated why—given all the nightclubs in the world—the problem-causing woman chose to enter his club.

Why *did* the woman choose his nightclub? Yes, as I have discussed in the previous section of this book, she made the decision to attend the nightclub in order to satisfy some basic need, but why did she choose *his* club? How did she go about making that decision and determining that visiting Keenen's nightclub was a good thing to do? When I purchased that suit, how — intrinsically — did I determine that purchasing the suit was a good thing to do?

I believe that when people are confronted with a decision — if they are rational — they follow a rational decision-making process or a *rational routing routine*.

The Rational Routing Routine

The **Rational Routing Routine** (R3) is a simple decision-making model I developed which describes the process that rational people go through — whether consciously or subconsciously — to make meaningful decisions and to figure out the best path forward. There are three elements of the model which consists of five stages. The three *elements* of the R3 decision-making model include:

- A "Rational" element (an assumption of sanity)
- A "Routing" element (an assumption of logical progression)
- A "Routine" element (an assumption of consistency in problem solving)

The "Rational" element of the model suggests that people are basically mentally sane, exercise sound judgment and use common sense when confronting a problem or considering an approach to a conflict. A "problem," as I am using the term here, is defined as an unsatisfied need, something that creates discomfort, or something that prevents a person from achieving some optimal or desirable state. In this context, a problem can be as significant as a sky-diver's parachute failing to open when she is 12,500 feet above ground level, or as inconsequential as a person trying to figure out the answer to a frustrating riddle.

How, I'm sure you are wondering, could the act of trying to solve a riddle rise to the level of creating discomfort? Because man is basically ignorant, in the sense that there is so much about the world that we do not know. And the knowledge of our ignorance causes us to be incessantly curious and leaves us with an unquenchable thirst for knowledge; not knowing things makes us extremely uncomfortable.

Consider this: Imagine you are taking a relaxing wilderness vacation and you decide to rent a cabin for the week. You arrive at what you believe to be a one-bedroom cabin and notice that there appears to be a second room in the cabin; you assume there is another room because there is a door. The door is shut so you have no idea what is beyond it. You approach the door to investigate only to find that the door is locked. In this situation, every day that you are in that cabin you will be consumed by your curiosity regarding what is beyond that locked door.

Why? Do you hear the sound of what might be a grizzly bear behind the door, giving you a "legitimate" reason to be concerned? No. Do you smell smoke emanating from the room, giving you a "legitimate" reason to be concerned about what's on the other side of the door? No. Do you hear the voice of what sounds like a crazed maniac tied to a chair shouting, "Goddamnit! Untie me! Let me outta this room! I'm gonna kill somebody!"? No. Even though you are not faced with any of these understandably curiosity-inducing events, you nonetheless have a burning desire to know what the hell is behind that door.

Why would you allow your curiosity to eat at you for every waking moment of the entire week that you stay in that cabin? Because, as I said earlier, we human beings have an intrinsic curiosity borne of the fact that we hate not knowing things. It is actually symptomatic of the self-actualization need. And when we don't know something that we want to know, we hate it.

And yes, this curiosity-borne frustration can even manifest itself in something as trivial as not knowing the answer to a simple riddle. You disagree? Okay, let's give it a test. Answer the following simple riddle:

Why did an old lady always answer the door wearing her hat and coat?

If you do not already know the answer to this riddle then I'd be willing to bet that you will think about it every day for some period of time until you either figure out or find the answer, or until enough time passes and you naturally forget about it. If you cannot figure it out, the unknowing will make you so ... *uncomfortable*, that you will then resort to either looking it up on the Internet or asking your friends and family for help answering it; mark my word.

This is an example of how something so seemingly innocent and harmless can be considered a problem if it results in discomfort. The Rational element of the R3 model compels people to answer the following questions when faced with a decision that has to be made, a problem that has to be addressed, or an answer that has to be discovered:

- What issue must I resolve in order to be satisfied, happy, and/or fulfilled?
- Can the issue be resolved? How will I know that it has been resolved?
- Should I care to resolve it? If so, why should I care?
- What would be the value to me of addressing and resolving the issue? What is the purpose?
- What is the downside or consequence if I do not resolve the issue?
- How will I know that the resolution would be an improvement?

The "Routing" element of the Rational Routing Routine model suggests that a person's thought process follows a logical course and is sequential (one action followed by another). We identify a possible course of action toward making a decision and/or resolving a problem, consider our available options, and then consider the implications and possible outcomes of our desired action before we actually engage in it. And, as rational beings, we will only engage in those actions whose expected outcome is favorable.

After we engage in the first action, we will then determine the next possible action we should take, consider the outcomes likely associated with this action, ultimately decide which course of action to take, and then take the action. We will repeat this process until we come to a resolution of the problem (the satisfaction of a need).

Routing involves cause-and-effect considerations, ruling out coincidence as much as possible. Cause-and-effect supposes that if you do "A" then "B" will happen as a direct result of having done "A". And if you do not do "A" then "B" will not happen. Coincidence, on the other hand, supposes that if you do "C" then "D" happens. However, "D" could have happened even if you did not do "C". Therefore, the "D" event would be considered a coincidence because it randomly happened to occur right after you did "C", and its occurrence was not related to the "C" event.

An example of causation (cause-and-effect) is turning on a light switch: when you flip a light switch, the light comes on. And if you flipped the light switch 100 times, the light would come on 100 times. The light coming on (the effect) is a direct result of you having turned on the light switch (the cause for the light coming on). And it is safe to assume that, if you did not turn on the light switch, then the light would not go on.

An example of a *coincidence* is if you blow your nose and a Jehovah's Witness knocks on your door. Whether you blew your nose or not, the Jehovah's Witness would have knocked on your door *anyway* — trust me — so the act of blowing your nose had nothing to with the Jehovah's Witness showing up at your house. Only a crazy person would believe that his or her nose caused that to happen. This is why one of the conditions of the R3 model — the Rational element — holds that people are *sane*.

The sequential nature of the Routing element holds that once we take an action, we expect that the outcome of the action (an outcome we predicted would occur before we took the action) actually occurs. If it does, then we consider the next action to engage in that will get us another step closer to resolving an issue or satisfying a need. The Routing element of the R3 model for decision-making compels people to ask the following questions once they have made the decision to pursue the solution to a problem:

- How do I get from my current state to my desired state? What series of actions will most likely lead to a resolution of the identified issue?
- If I do "A," then what would happen ("B")? Is the possible outcome of that action desirable?
- Will successfully engaging in the action get me one step closer to a resolution of the identified issue?

"DAMN, I'VE GOTTA PEE"

The third element of the R3 model—the "Routine" element—acknowledges that people engage in the rational process of problem resolution on a consistent basis and follow a similar (if not the same) process each time—and without giving much thought to exactly *how* they do it.

An example of a process-based routine that we perform without giving it much thought is when we wake up in the morning and go to the bathroom to pee. Think about how the routine technically works: While you were asleep, your bladder reached its functional capacity of retaining urine. When you woke up, you felt the discomfort of your full bladder (a basic physiological need for elimination) so you sat up, put your feet on the floor, stood up, stumbled to the bathroom, located the toilet (usually), removed the necessary clothing (usually), and initiated the voluntary voiding. In other words, you peed.

Of the 3,000 times that you urinate each year have you ever, I mean EVER, once thought about all of the steps involved in the morning pee routine? I would bet that you have not. If you are like me, your morning routine goes something like this: The alarm clock (either mechanical or human) goes off and wakes you up. As you lay there, dreading the thought of getting out of your warm bed, you realize: "Damn. I've gotta pee." You stumble to the bathroom, yawn, throw your head back, and let it flow. While you are standing or sitting there basking in the relief and comfort offered by this most prehistoric of human bodily functions, are you really thinking about how the muscle of your bladder is being stimulated by the nervous system fibers from your lumbar spinal cord? No! The only thing you are thinking is, "Ahhhhh! That feels good!"

Urinating is an action that we take on a regular basis without ever thinking exactly how we do it. The same holds true for the routine of simple problem-solving proposed by my Rational Routing Routine model: We engage in the stages of this routine without explicitly thinking about the complexities of the process that we are following; it happens naturally.

When we establish that a need must be satisfied, we will either decide to engage in a behavior that satisfies the need (because we determine intrinsically that it is in our self-interest to do so), or to *not* engage in the behavior because we determine that engaging in the activity is not in our self-interest. Whichever course of action we decide upon—to engage in the need-satisfying behavior or not—I contend that we will, perhaps unconsciously, follow a logical process such as the Rational Routing Routine to arrive at that decision.

Elements *of the* Rational Routing Routine Summarized

R3 Element ▶ Rational Consideration

Rational Consideration is the expectation that people are basically mentally sane, exercise sound judgment and use common sense when confronting a problem or considering an approach to a conflict. We acknowledge that we have a basic need (which can be considered a problem) that must be satisfied and we determine whether or not the need *can* be satisfied.

Our Rational Consideration forces us to answer the questions:

- What issue must I resolve to be satisfied, happy, and/or fulfilled?
- Can the issue be resolved? How will I know that it has been resolved?
- Should I care to resolve it? If so, why should I care?
- What would be the value to me of addressing and resolving the issue? What is the purpose?
- What is the downside or consequence if I do not resolve the issue?
- How will I know that the resolution would be an improvement?

R3 Element ▶ Decision-Making Routing ("A" to "Z")

A person's thought process follows a logical course (route) and is sequential (one action followed by another; getting from "A" to "Z") in that we identify a possible course of action toward making a decision and/or resolving a problem, consider our available options, and then consider the implications and possible outcomes of our desired action before we actually engage in it; as rational beings, we will only engage in actions that have a favorable expected outcome.

Our decision-making thought process forces us to ask ourselves the questions:

- How do I get from my current state to my desired state? What series of actions will most likely lead to a resolution of the identified issue?

- If I do "A" then what would happen ("B")? Is the possible outcome of that action desirable?

- Will successfully engaging in the action get me one step closer to a resolution of the identified issue?

R3 Element ▶ Problem Resolution Routine

People engage in the rational, logical process of problem resolution on a consistent basis and follow a similar (if not the same) general process each time we do so—and we do it without giving much thought to how exactly we do it.

The six stages of the *R3 Decision-Making Model* are described below:

Stage 1: Problem Identification: Basic Need Acknowledgement

When making a decision pursuant to a goal, it is important to acknowledge that there is a problem to be addressed and/or a need to be satisfied. If you cannot acknowledge that a problem exists or that there is a need that must be satisfied, then it will be quite difficult to make the best decisions about a path forward.

Stage 2: Determine: Can the Need be Satisfied?

If the need is unsatisfiable, then there is no point pursuing a course of action; the same holds true for problems. For this reason, it is important to clearly identify a need or define a problem before attempting to satisfy and/or solve it.

Stage 3: Consider the Available Options

There are typically multiple options available to the decision-maker for satisfying a need or resolving a problem. It is important to identify all of the available options (often presented as initiatives) before deciding on a course of action.

Stage 4: Consider the Expected Benefits and/or Consequences

For every available option, there are numerous benefits or consequences associated with it. Choose wisely.

Stage 5: Determine The Path to the Benefits (Actions)

Once a decision has been made based on the available options, the next step is to determine the specific actions and tasks that must be executed/followed in order to deliver on the chosen option or initiative.

Stage 6: Resolution: Resolve the Issue (Need Satisfaction)

If the decision-making process was executed following the constructs of the Rational Routing Routine, there is a high probability that the need will have been satisfied and the problem resolved.

The relationship between the Rational Routing Routine and the associated six stages of the decision-making model is depicted below.

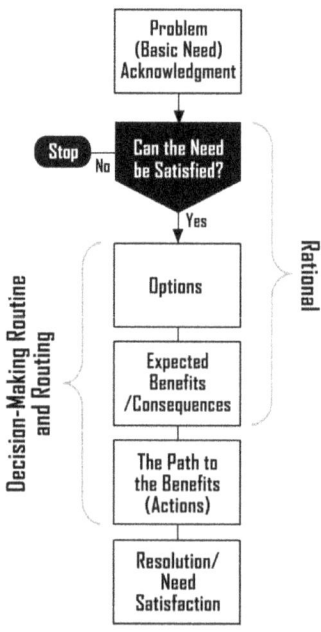

Because—as I believe—all of our actions are self-interested and aimed at satisfying some basic need, when I purchased the $5,000 suit I was more than likely trying to satisfy an *esteem need* (seeking feelings of self-confidence, strength, and the respect of others). Looking back, I realize that when I purchased the suit I followed the R3 model to arrive at my decision—though I was unaware that I was actually following a routine. My R3 process for purchasing the suit went something like this:

Question	Subconscious Answer
What issue must I resolve to be satisfied, happy, and/or fulfilled?	I wanted to satisfy my need for additional self-confidence and the respect of others.
Can the issue be resolved? How will I know that it has been resolved?	Yes, the issue can be resolved. I would know that the issue had been resolved when I wore the suit in front of an audience, felt the added confidence brought on by wearing the suit, and received acknowledgement from the audience that I looked rather snappy wearing the suit.
Should I care to satisfy the need? If so, why should I care?	Because I don't believe that any of my existing suits would have given me the same feeling of confidence as the $5,000 suit (okay, so maybe that's a reach. But there is a modicum of truth to it).

Question	Subconscious Answer
What would be the value to me of addressing and resolving the issue? What is the purpose?	The purpose is to give me an added level of self-confidence and demonstrate to the audience that I am the epitome of professionalism. This would enable my keynote delivery to be even more effective and, as a result, create additional opportunities for me.
What is the downside or consequence if I do not resolve the issue?	If I purchased the suit, wore it, and didn't feel any increased confidence, I would view the purchase as wasteful.
How will I know that the resolution would be an improvement?	If, when wearing that suit, I felt better on stage than when wearing any of my other suits, then the suit would have resulted in an improvement of my comfort, confidence level, and performance.
How do I get from my current state to my desired state? What series of actions will most likely lead to a resolution of the identified issue?	Buy the suit, make sure that it is impeccably tailored, and wear it.
If I do "A" then what would ultimately happen? Is the possible outcome of that action desirable?	If I purchased the suit ("A"), ensured a perfect fit ("B"), complemented the suit with the appropriate accoutrements ("C"), and wore the suit to the seminar ("D"), my confidence level and the audience's acceptance of my appropriateness of attire would lead to a desirable outcome.

The Rational Routing Routine not only assists us in our efforts to satisfy obvious physiological or basic needs, such as hunger and esteem, but it also helps us to arrive at the resolution option that is in our best interest. In addition—whether we are aware of it or not—the routine can also be followed when resolving minor discomforts or problems. As I wrote earlier in this chapter, we humans hate the fact that we are ignorant and our ignorance makes us curious about anything for which we have no answer. This not-knowing leads to frustration which creates a small problem. When this occurs, our desperate need to find an answer to the unknown is revealed as an actualization need for *understanding*, and can manifest itself as discontentedness and restlessness. Even an understanding need as insignificant as the aforementioned riddle of *the old lady answering the door* can be resolved following the R3 model.

Here is another riddle to consider (I do not want to use the riddle of *the old lady answering the door* for this example because I want you, the reader, to feel the frustration that we all experience when we don't know the answer to something which we desperately want to know):

There is an exclusive, after-hour speakeasy that is the hottest ticket in town. However, it is very difficult to get into. The only way to get in is to know the secret code. One day, a newcomer got in line to try to gain access to the club. There were two other men in front of him in line. The first man walked up to the door and the doorman said one word: "Twelve." The first man replied,

"Six." He was admitted into the club. When the second man approached the door, the doorman said, "Six," and the second man replied, "Three." He, too, was admitted into the club. The newcomer saw the process followed by the other two men and thought he had it figured out. He walked up to the door and the doorman said, "Ten." The newcomer replied, "Five." The doorman angrily slammed the door in his face and did not let him in. What should the newcomer have said?

Question	Subconscious Answer
What issue must I resolve to be satisfied, happy, and/or fulfilled?	My esteem need for understanding. My ignorance-borne curiosity is eating at me.
Can the issue be resolved? How will I know that it has been resolved?	Yes, the issue can and will be resolved when I learn the answer and my curiosity is satisfied.
Should I care to satisfy the need? If so, why should I care?	Because not knowing the answer to the riddle will continue to annoy me and make me uncomfortable.
What would be the value to me of addressing and resolving the issue? What is the purpose?	Discovering the answer will satisfy my need for understanding, reduce my anxiety level, and make me feel good.

"DAMN, I'VE GOTTA PEE"

Question	Subconscious Answer
What is the downside or consequence if I do not resolve the issue?	If the issue goes unresolved, I will experience continued discomfort whenever I think about this or any other stupid riddle.
How will I know that the resolution would be an improvement?	Because knowing the answer will satisfy my curiosity and my need for understanding.
How do I get from my current state to my desired state? What series of actions will most likely lead to a resolution of the identified issue?	I will either need to go to the Internet and look the answer up or ask my family and friends to help me solve the riddle.
If I do "A" then what would ultimately happen? Is the possible outcome of that action desirable?	If I log onto the Internet ("A") and perform a search for the riddle ("B"), I will learn that the secret code is the number of letters in the doorman's word and that newcomer should have said "Three" because the word "Ten" (the doorman's word) contains "three" letters (outcome "C").

Pigs' Feet and Crème Brulee

The Rational Routing Routine
as a Logical Process

In one sense, *logic* is the application of reasoned thought as opposed to irrational thought. Because logic also relates to the relationship and interdependence of a series of events, applying logic to our thought processes helps us make sound judgments and good-sense decisions, as well as formulate conclusions. In this sense, logic and The Rational Routing Routine are aligned in that both are approaches to arriving at sound decisions. Logic is an underpinning of The Rational Routing Routine, helping us get from "A" to "Z" in a rational manner. It enables us to arrive at a resolution by experiencing as few pitfalls and bad decisions as possible.

So how does the R3 model square up with a logical thinking process? If the concepts are in relative alignment, then we can rest more assured that the subconscious process we follow toward the resolution of a problem or the satisfaction of a basic need is grounded in common sense and thoughtfulness, leading to outcomes that are more attuned to our self-interests than not.

Logical thinking is the process by which one uses reasoning consistently to come to a conclusion. Logical thinking—whether we are consciously aware of it or not—helps us make responsible (moral, beneficial, and useful) decisions. We do this by incorporating the following tools into the decision-making process: our desired goals (outcomes); our unfulfilled needs; the activities or actions we can engage in to satisfy the needs; and the expected effects or consequences of these actions if we choose to engage in them.

• **Goals**. A *goal* is the intended result of whatever a person is engaged in. It is a general statement of a broad, intended outcome. For example, a woman who is trying to lose weight might be doing so because she wants to look "good" for her 20-year high school reunion. In this example, the woman's goal might be defined as: *I want to look good for my high school reunion* (however she defines "good"). To take it a step further, the woman could choose to apply a specific, time-bound weight-loss *objective* toward her goal of "looking good." She might define an objective as: *I want to lose 15 pounds over the next 30 days*. The logic is that by losing the 15 pounds, she will look "good" and, therefore, will have accomplished her identified goal.

I am a firm believer that everything we do could be done more efficiently if we first determined what we are ultimately trying to accomplish, and then followed a logical approach to arrive at that goal.

• **Unfulfilled Needs**. As I wrote previously, all human behavior is aimed toward the satisfaction of basic human needs. When a need is unfulfilled, people's actions will be directed toward fulfilling the need until the need is satisfied. And when it is, people will then aim their behavior toward fulfilling another need, perhaps a different basic need or a subsequent-level need for safety, love, esteem, or actualization. Imagine, for example, that a man has been lost at sea for two weeks with no food or water; he is fading fast. Suddenly, he washes ashore and when he opens his eyes, he sees three things: a suitcase filled with $1,000,000 in cash, a scantily-clad supermodel waving "come hither," and a Thanksgiving feast with all the trimmings—including an ice-cold pitcher of water. Which of these three things do you think the man will rush toward first? The smart money says that the man would attack the Thanksgiving feast and the cold water. If so—and logic would dictate that it is—then the man's actions would support the contention that physiological or basic needs (food, water, etc.) must be satisfied before the man can even begin to focus on his other needs for love (the scantily-clad supermodel) and esteem (the suitcase containing $1,000,000).

• **Actions**. The actions in which a person engages will be based on the things that must be accomplished to satisfy the person's unfulfilled needs. They answer the question: What steps must I take in order to satisfy my unfulfilled needs and how will I do it? Let's say, for example, that the man who was lost at sea and eventually reached the shore noticed that a crazed wild boar was standing in front of the Thanksgiving feast table and that a rifle was within arms-reach. The man would decide that, in order to satisfy his hunger (his unfulfilled need), he would first have to kill the wild boar (an objective and the action).

He would then determine that the way he will execute this required action is to use the rifle to shoot the wild boar (his execution of the *action*).

• **Expected Effects of the Actions**. When thinking logically about engaging in an activity, we should always consider the expected or likely effects of our engagement in the activity and the consequences or benefits that will result from this action. For instance, the aforementioned woman who is trying to lose weight for her high school reunion might consider taking a short-cut and ingesting the stimulant drug Methamphetamine (also known as "Speed" or "Ice"); this was not uncommon among some people I knew growing up. When the woman considers the expected effects of ingesting the drug (her action) she will find that, on the positive side, she would lose weight rapidly, she would have intensified feelings of sexual desire, and she would experience increased strength and renewed energy. The negative effects, however, could include depression, hallucinations, delusions, and lung, liver and kidney damage. After evaluating the expected effects of her actions—if she is rational—the woman would likely conclude that the risks and potential negative effects of "speeding" the weight off far outweigh any positive benefits she could expect to receive, and she would therefore decide not to engage in that action.

When comparing The Rational Routing Routine to a logical thinking process, we find that the R3 model is, indeed, logical at its foundation (see the diagram below). This suggests that when we make decisions—conscious or not—based on our own self-interests toward the satisfaction of a basic need, the decisions we ultimately arrive at are logical ones.

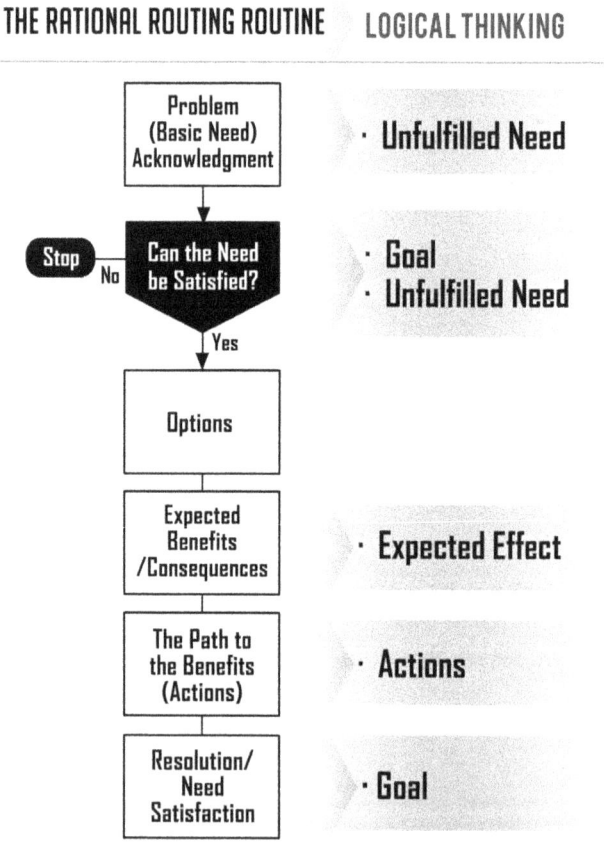

"DAMN, I'VE GOTTA PEE"

I know ... I know ... I know: Sometimes, even when we are thinking logically, we still may decide to do something despite the fact that it appears to be "illogical" (or irrational and not based on reason or fact). For example: Traditional crème brulee (translation: "burnt cream"), the fancy French dessert, is primarily made of heavy cream, egg yolks, and sugar; all truly heart-healthy ingredients (I say sarcastically). Fact: A single serving of crème brulee contains 27.5 grams of fat and 270 calories. Comparatively, a McDonald's Big Mac® hamburger contains 29 grams of fat and 260 calories. Pretty similar. Before I continue I want to go on the record as saying that I am in no way one of those calorie-counting, "I-can't-believe-you're-gonna-eat-that!" wahoos who have nothing better to do with their time than think that everyone else should only eat what *they* eat. Frankly, I couldn't care less about what people eat.

Now back to the crème brulee example.

So, that crème brulee—the same crème brulee for which you paid $26 at that swanky French restaurant and is comprised of nothing but heavy cream, egg yolks, and sugar, and contains the same amount of fat as a Big Mac®—is worse for you than a $2 plate of *pigs' feet*! Yes, *pigs' feet*! "Slop walkers," "Jelly knuckles," "Trotters," "Pork stands," PIGS' FEET, for chrissakes!

So is there really any logical reason to eat crème brulee? Not really. Is there any rational reason to drink coffee? Who knows. And was there any rational reason for me to buy that expensive suit considering that I already had plenty of other suits which were—but for the company of a few moths—hanging neglected in my closet? Nope. So does that mean we shouldn't do these things because the decision to do them is not a *logical* one? No. We act in our self-interest when we satisfy our basic needs, and our desire for these things indicates that we have an unfulfilled need. And because doing these things (even if it's eating pigs' feet) satisfies the need, makes us feel good, brings us some measure of pleasure, and makes us happy, then—as I contend throughout this book—we should just say "What the f**k!" and do them anyway. Because, in the end, these self-interested acts are aimed at satisfying some basic need and will, ultimately, be good for us, our families, and society.

So logic, reason, and rationality help us choose among available options and courses of action. These factors help us make the "best" decisions ("best" defined as those choices that satisfy our basic needs and goals most efficiently and with the least disruption or discomfort), but not necessarily the decisions that satisfy the need in the progression in which needs—according to Maslow—are supposed to be satisfied.

Pleasure and Pain

The decision-making process and the expected effects of one's actions introduce the concepts of *pleasure*, *pain*, and *risk*, which can have a significant impact on the choices we make and the outcomes and consequences of those choices and resulting actions.

Pleasure

Every day, we are presented with choices and, when choosing among available options, we fundamentally make decisions to engage in an activity or follow a course of action that will result in the satisfaction of a basic need. Assuming we can act of our own free will with no external influence or interference, we will act in our self-interest and decide to engage in those activities that provide us with enjoyment and satisfaction, or *pleasure*. This is logical.

Suppose, for example, you attended an important business luncheon at which they served your favorite dessert: homemade apple pie topped with vanilla ice cream. Yum! You eat the pie and it is truly the *best* Pie à la Mode you have ever had. You want seconds. However, because you are seated at a table with your boss and some important clients, you don't ask for another piece of the pie because you're concerned with how you would be perceived by the other people at your table. This is an example of how external influences (your boss and clients) can impact your decision-making. This is also an example of what psychoanalysts refer to as the *reality principle*, which describes how a person will choose to defer the gratification or pleasure brought by a desirable activity (eating a second helping of the Pie à la Mode) when circumstantial reality (sitting at a table with your boss and clients) disallows its immediate gratification.

If, however, you were at home with your family having dinner on some random Tuesday night and that same pie and ice cream were on your dinner table, you would not hesitate to have seconds—or even thirds—because you would not be subjected to those external influences you faced at the business luncheon. In the latter case, you could act of your own interference-free will and the decision you would make would be to have more of the pie and ice cream. You would choose to engage in the activity that brought you pleasure.

Verbing the Noun

You may be wondering: What about external influences that, over time, have lasting influences on peoples' behavior? Sometimes these influences are so great that a person becomes conflicted over that which is logical and that which—although not logical—has been instilled in the person to the point where the person is more inclined to engage in the externally-influenced behavior than the logical behavior, even when the externally-influenced behavior conflicts with the person's intrinsic desire to do otherwise? Take pork consumption, for example.

Religious restrictions on the consumption of pork are a tradition that dates back thousands of years across many religions, including Judaism, Islam, and even among Christians (Seventh-day Adventists). In *The Holy Bible King James Version: 1611 Edition*, Leviticus 11:7-8 states: *And the swine, though he divide the hoof, and be clovenfooted, yet he cheweth not the cud; he [is] unclean to you. Of their flesh shall ye not eat, and their carcase shall ye not touch; they [are] unclean to you.*

"DAMN, I'VE GOTTA PEE"

So if you are a person who has been raised to follow such religious laws since you were in diapers—and your family, friends, and fellow religious followers reinforced the forbidden-swine mantra every day—you would be less inclined to eat pork than a non-believer. James Baldwin, the famous American novelist, essayist, playwright, poet, and social critic once commented: "The paradox of education is precisely this—that as one begins to become conscious one begins to examine the society in which he is being educated." This statement describes what happens when many people become more learned, pursue higher education, or simply *grow up*. Over time, as you become more worldly, more rebellious, and you begin to question *everything*, you might start to read such books as *Letter to a Christian Nation* by American author Sam Harris, or *The GOD Delusion* by evolutionary biologist Richard Dawkins. Eventually, you might come to question the logic and rationality of a restriction on the consumption of pork. And it doesn't help when you start joining your friends for breakfast at iHop and you smell that incredible smell of pork bacon ... Ahhh, *bacon!* ... and witness the way your friends devour that forbidden pork bacon. At that point, an internal struggle will ensue between your rational inner-self and the external influences imposed on you since you were a child. Next, one of two things will happen: either you will succumb to the external influences and continue to abstain from eating pork or you will say "What the f**k!" and eat some bacon.

I have a friend who, for religious reasons, does not

eat pork; he considers pork to be on the same scale as poison. One day, I asked my friend why he doesn't eat pork, and his response was that he is instructed not to do so in his holy book. When I asked why his holy book instructs not to eat pork, he said the reason is because pigs are filthy and carry trichina—which can cause a foodborne disease called trichinosis—and other maladies. I replied that, back when the holy book was written, people who consumed pork could become ill but that, since then, consumers have learned techniques for the proper handling, storage, preparation, and cooking of pork. As a result, the meat is about as safe to eat as beef. I went on to say that if the reason for pork's restriction is its safety, and if pork safety is no longer the same issue it was thousands of years ago, then why is it still banned? My friend (again) replied that it's banned because pigs are filthy. I asked what he thought of medieval Jewish philosopher Moses Maimonides' assertion that the principal reason why the religious law forbids swine's flesh is because the pig's habits and its food are very dirty and loathsome. In other words, another issue that doesn't impact the final pork product. My friend finally said, "Man, I don't know why we're not supposed to eat pork. It's in the [holy book]. But I must admit: when I smell pork spare ribs cooking on the grill, it's very tempting!"

This is an example of external influences affecting a person's behavior to the point that the externally-influenced-mandate became the norm for my friend, even though, if he had his druthers, he would eat grilled pork spare ribs.

"DAMN, I'VE GOTTA PEE"

There is an activity, however, on which external influences fail to have an impact once a person reaches puberty, and that is *masturbation*. Growing up, I remember a story being told that masturbation lead to blindness in boys. But why would anyone warn against masturbation? That's like telling people: when you are hungry, don't cook your own meal in your own kitchen, but instead, always go to a restaurant to eat.

Some people believe that the Christian Bible suggests the punishment of death for the "wicked" act. In The New International Version of the Bible (a version that provides an easy to understand English translation of the scriptures), Genesis 38:8-10 states: *"Then Judah said to Onan, 'Lie with your brother's wife and fulfill your duty to her as a brother-in-law to produce offspring for your brother.' But Onan knew that the offspring would not be his; so whenever he lay with his brother's wife he spilled his semen on the ground to keep from producing offspring for his brother. What he did was wicked in the Lord's sight; so he put him to death also."*

Put to death for *masturbating*?! If death actually came to all who masturbate, there would only be 15,000,000 people left in the United States—all women—and roughly 300 million people—the population of the United States—left in the entire *world*. And what about infants who masturbate? Yes, you read it correctly: Infant boys and girls *do* masturbate, often when they get bored or tired. Should *they* be put to death, too, for engaging in a normal human behavior that they don't understand but do it nonetheless?

Cultural taboos such as this make people, especially women, feel that masturbating and self-gratification are somehow wrong—some feel guilt or shame just for thinking about it. Guys have absolutely no problem self-gratifying; we have been known to do it while driving a car through midtown Manhattan in rush hour traffic while listening to Barry Manilow and sipping a Slurpee...uh... or so I've been told. Women, on the other hand, often feel reluctant to masturbate. That's unfortunate because, in addition to providing pleasure, masturbation offers many benefits to women, including: helping prevent cervical infections; helping relieve urinary tract infections; improving cardiovascular health; lowering the risk of type-2 diabetes; curing insomnia; improving one's mood; and relieving stress. Masturbation may also strengthen the sexual relationship with a partner. So, if for no other reason than to receive those wonderful health, psychological, and emotional benefits, I encourage all women to 'housebreak the cat'.

Think about it this way: By masturbating, you would satisfy a love need and, at the same time, provide yourself with a pleasurable experience. This pleasure will make you feel good, and when you feel good, you're happier. When you are happy, your happiness spreads to your loved ones (remember: masturbation strengthens the sexual relationship with a partner), and they, too, will be happy, and their happiness will spread to others (hopefully, not their *sexual* happiness). And when more people are happy, people cooperate, leading to increased productivity, development, and overall strength in the community and, ultimately, the world. And it's all because you decided to act in your self-interest—spurning the external influences—and provide yourself with pleasure.

So the next time you're feeling libidinous and your partner is nowhere to be found (or you'd simply like to go it alone), but you feel guilty about masturbating because those grade school nuns laid a serious guilt trip on you about touching yourself when you were in the third grade, just say "What the f**k!" and go for it: Jill off, box the bald-headed clown, badger the witness, slap-box the one-eyed champ, Pat the Robertson, smoke hooch with Reagan, torture the political prisoner, fire the Surgeon-General, verb the noun, Mork the Mindy, comfort the Bishop, or wave the writ of Habeas Corpus to the Sheriff of Nottingham, because, in the end, acting in your self-interest and masturbating will turn out to be good for both you and your loved ones.

Masturbation is not a sin; it provides pleasure. *Pleasure* is a mental state that we experience as positive, enjoyable, or worth seeking. It is the enjoyment or satisfaction (of a basic need) that is derived from engaging in certain activities, such as eating pie à la mode, for example. And when we can act of our own free will, we are motivated to behave in ways that produce pleasurable feelings and thoughts, and avoid painful ones. This is an idea consistent with what Austrian neurologist Sigmund Freud referred to as the *pleasure principle*.

The pleasure principle is a psychoanalytic concept that describes how people will seek to engage in activities that bring us pleasure and avoid suffering as we try to satisfy our biological and physiological needs (our *basic needs*). For example, when I'm hungry I find pleasure in eating French fries so I seek them out. But I find it painful to eat phall curry (the hottest curry one can eat) so I avoid it. Freud found that the good feelings we associate with certain behaviors are reinforcing, and the association of a stimulus with those feelings builds habits which facilitate our future decision-making process involving these stimuli. This means that whenever we are faced with a choice that involves the stimulus which made us feel good in the past, it will be easier and faster for us to make that decision because we learned that engaging in the activity that previously brought us pleasure is likely to lead to another positive (pleasurable) outcome. Contrarily, if we engaged in an activity involving a stimulus that was associated with pain, we would avoid those activities in the future.

Pain

Here's an interesting conundrum: What about people who derive "pleasure" from pain? Such people are often referred to as *masochists*. Masochism is context-dependent (relative), meaning that masochists don't simply enjoy all types of pain or painful experiences, only certain kinds and within certain situations. In an *absolute* sense, for instance, puncturing your skin with a sewing needle hurts, regardless of who you are. If you asked 100 people what it would feel like if you were to stick a needle into their back, every person would say that it would *hurt*. Why? Because our experience with being stuck by needles tells us that it results in a painful feeling.

In a *relative* sense, however, there are certain cases where sticking a pin into a person's back would bring a sense of pleasure—think *acupuncture*. Similarly, several years ago I received a back massage that was actually quite painful. The masseuse grappled with my back as if she were kneading dough to make bread—and it hurt! But then a funny thing happened. As I headed home after the massage, the pain in my back and shoulders that had resulted from the masseuse's kneading actually began to feel soothing and it helped me to relax. Even though it still "hurt," it felt good at the same time. Weird. In that situation, pain was context-dependent.

Freud said that people become masochistic as a way of regulating their desire to dominate others. The desire to submit, he said, arises from guilt feelings over that desire to dominate. According to Roy Baumeister, a professor of psychology at Case Western Reserve University, masochism is a set of techniques for helping people temporarily lose their normal identity. He argues that our Western culture places such high demands on people that the demands ultimately increase the stress associated with trying to live up to society's—and our own—expectations of us. The stress, he says, makes the thought of "escaping" an appealing one; it's a way for people to forget themselves. This is the essence of escape theory, suggesting that escaping one's self is a major reason why people turn to sadomasochism (S&M)—the giving and/or receiving of pleasure, often sexual, from acts involving the infliction or reception of pain or humiliation. In most cases, the satisfaction gained from S&M is not simply about sex, but rather a total emotional release.

We often hear stories about how many submissive practitioners of S&M are high-powered CEO's of major corporations. In the office or the boardroom, they are in control, demanding, dominating. But when he engages in S&M, the CEO becomes submissive and peaceful, as though he's injected heroin into his veins. And each time the dominatrix doles out pain, the CEO tenses up for a brief moment and then falls into a deeper state of calm and pleasure. This is an example of how a person with so many expectations of performance placed upon them could seek to escape and, ultimately, turn to something like S&M, drugs, or alcohol as a means to compensate for a stimulus deficit.

In my opinion, if "pain" is the result of physical suffering—that feeling we experience when we say something *hurts*—and if *pleasure* is the mental state we experience when something's enjoyable, then a masochist's "pain" is actually "pleasure" for them. So, by definition, are the feelings they experience when they participate in these activities "pain," or simply their version of *pleasure*? Probably a little bit of both. But since people seek out pleasure-inducing stimuli based on experience, and the masochist seeks out the dominatrix's whipping, then it could be argued that—to the masochist—the feeling that results from being whipped is pleasure. And in that sense, masochists are just like everyone else who seek "pleasurable" experiences to satisfy our basic needs.

"DAMN, I'VE GOTTA PEE"

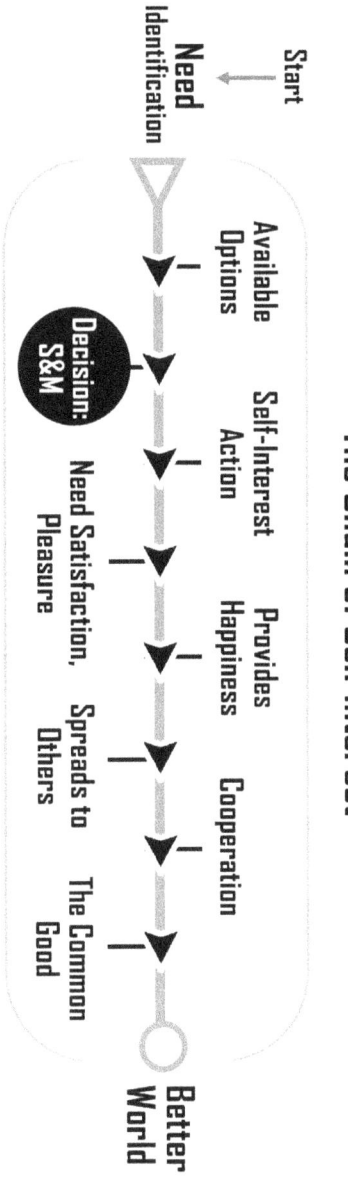

CHAPTER 06
RISK

When making decisions based on the possible choices, options, or courses of action available to us, if we are rational, we will consider the possible effects and outcomes of a decision before choosing a particular course of action. The possible outcomes of our decisions will either be positive (good), neutral (no impact), or negative (bad). Naturally, we would all like for every one of the options available to us to result in positive outcomes, but the reality is that many—if not most—of the decisions we are faced with could lead to unfavorable outcomes which would negatively impact the decision-maker. This introduces the concept of *risk*—the possibility of hazard, misfortune, danger, or loss—into the decision-making process.

In a 2003 survey of a representative sample of people aged fifteen and older, 47% of the respondents agreed with the following statement: "I am willing to take big chances to get what I want out of life." So about half of the population is willing to take "big" risks to make themselves happy or to improve their station in life. When you consider that the respondents were not simply a bunch of energy-drink-consuming, Madden Football-playing, X-Games-watching, young punks, but also included middle-aged and elderly people, it suggests that there is something inherent in us that disposes us to taking risks.

When talking about risk and risky behavior, it is reasonable to consider whether risk-taking is a 'normal,' 'acceptable,' or 'rational' behavior—especially since nearly 50% of people are willing to take "big" risks and risk inherently involves a loss of some kind. However, while I will not delve into a discussion of risk normality or risk acceptability, I will discuss the rationality of risk-taking in its appropriate context throughout this book.

Back in 9th grade Biology class, I learned that human beings are supposed to be risk-avoiders and safety-seekers; it's necessary for the survival of the species. And since all risk involves some loss, one would think that people acting rationally would avoid risk at all costs. But risk-taking is rational under certain situations. For instance, if a knife-wielding burglar broke into your house and threatened to go into your kid's room, you would probably make the risky decision to attack the knife-wielding burglar in order to protect your family—even though there is a big risk that you could be stabbed by the burglar in the process. Everyone would agree that in this situation, it is not only *rational* for you to accept the risk of attacking the man with the knife, but it is also your obligation to do so.

This example of the burglar would dispel the notion that people are naturally risk avoiders or "Zero-risk man." John Adams, professor of geography, University College, London, England, opines that risk-avoidance is but one aspect of the human character, and that another aspect of the human character—"Dice man"—is risk-*taking*. Assuming that Adams's assertion is valid (which I believe it is), then how would we describe the parent protecting their kid from the burglar? Are they a natural risk-taker, or does their *situation* and circumstance necessitate that they take the risk?

I believe that risk tolerance falls along a scale where, at one end of the continuum, there are people who actively seek risks (a "risk-seeker") and, at the other end, are the people who want nothing to do with risky situations ("risk-avoiders"). And somewhere between these two extremes are people who will engage in a risky situation if compelled to ("risk-accepters") and people who are willing to accept risks when the payoff is stimulus or excitement ("risk-takers"). And in my opinion—an opinion based solely on what I think rather than exhaustive research—the majority of people are risk-acceptors, followed by risk-avoiders, and then risk-takers, leaving risk-seekers as the smallest percentage of the population.

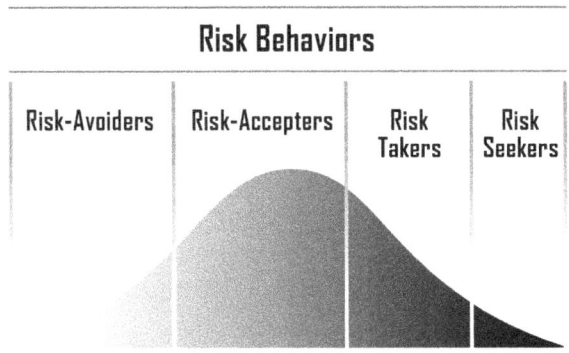

So, if I am at all close in my categorization, nearly everyone engages or would engage in activities involving risk at some point in our lives if compelled. And since most people are rational beings, then accepting risk and engaging in risky activities is rational depending on the situation or circumstance. The challenge arises in assessing the risks that confront us and making the best decision based on, among other factors, the expected level of risk associated with a decision and our willingness to accept it or our ability to forestall or mitigate the risk.

In order to forestall or mitigate the potential risks and negative consequences associated with a decision, the rational person will assess these factors (if "A" then "B") by following a risk routine that includes:

- Identifying the potential risks associated with each possible outcome of a decision
- Assessing the risks to determine their magnitude or impact

- Planning resolution actions should the risk situation occur
- Ongoing monitoring of the potential risks that could still occur after a decision is made
- Developing a risk contingency plan should a risk situation occur with a hazardous effect

By engaging in this risk assessment routine, the decision-maker can identify and evaluate the possible negative consequences of a particular course of action, take the necessary actions to prevent the risk from occurring, and put plans in place to lessen the impact of a negative outcome should it occur after a decision is made.

Often when we make decisions to pursue a particular course of action, the riskier options have the most appeal to us, and we have to determine whether or not the potential risk is worth the value that we derive from the action. For example, skiers get so much enjoyment out of skiing that they are willing to accept the risk of enduring an ABC-*Wide-World-of-Sports*-Vinko-Bogataj-"agony of defeat" type of spill often associated with the sport of skiing. In this example, the *expected utility* value of skiing —given the probability of a risky and uncertain outcome —is so high that the decision-maker believes the value of going skiing far exceeds the risks involved and, therefore, makes the decision to take that course of action.

RISK

The Expected Utility Theory of decision-making suggests that, given the two scenarios outlined in the table below, the rational person would choose to play poker (option A) after weighing the value of the outcome against the probability that the outcome will occur.

Activity	Potential Winnings	Probability of Winning	Potential Losses	Probability of Losing
(A) Play Poker	$1,000	25%	$250	10%
(B) Play Craps	$1,500	10%	$750	75%

The basic idea is that, when we make decisions that involve risk (e.g. skiing), we assess the probability or likelihood of experiencing the risk outcome of the action (falling and breaking bones), weigh it against the value we will derive from the action (the exhilaration of barreling down a hill of packed snow at 20 mph on skis), and make a decision based on the choice that we believe outweighs the other. In this case, the skier would decide that falling is a cost of experiencing the enjoyment of skiing, rather than an uncompensated loss—falling down the slope without having an opportunity to ski.

But why do we even make decisions that are considered "risky," especially when the consequences can be hazardous? When it comes to gambling, I can understand how *the greater the risk, the greater the return*, but why do we accept the potentially deadly risks that are associated with activities such as sky diving, heli-skiing, high-wire tightrope walking (have you seen the fascinating 2008 movie "Man on Wire"?), lion-taming, or having sex with strange men in the bathroom at the Washington D.C. Union Station's Amtrak train station? (More on that later). The answer appears to be *excitement*!

According to Marvin Zuckerman, a psychology professor from the University of Delaware, people who are willing to assume risk and engage in high-risk behaviors are *sensation-seekers* and have a *sensation-seeking trait*. They engage in both no-risk and risky behaviors because they are searching for a type of intrinsic reward or positive arousal. And economist & Stanford University professor Tibor Scitovsky hypothesized that modern man is developing a desire for excitement because scientific and economic progress have so diminished the hardships and hazards of everyday existence. Because man no longer needs to fight for survival, people are left with a *stimulus deficit* which they try to eliminate by seeking stimulation from risky—and often dangerous—activities.

Some will argue that risk isn't something we take on; it's who we are. Rather than think of risk-taking as a behavior choice, they argue, it should be viewed as an inherent personality trait where an individual willingly pursues novel and intense sensations. In this sense, risk-taking is expressed in the person who becomes bored with a set routine, who is impatient with people they consider dull. For them, it's much preferable having exciting people in their lives than reliable ones. This would explain why some women prefer "bad boys" to the clean-cut stable guy: Hanging out with bad boys is a form of risk that provides women with novel and intense sensations.

Biochemists in Israel found an association between sensation-seeking and one form of a gene that codes for a type of dopamine receptor. Dopamine is a brain neurotransmitter that is active in the brain's intrinsic reward and pleasure centers. The long form of the dopamine receptor-4 gene is found in a large majority of sensation-seekers, such as opiate drug abusers. Scientists believe there are probably other genes as well that contribute to this personality trait. The implication? Risk-taking associated with sensation-seeking provides the risk-taker with a sense of pleasure.

While risk-taking has negative connotations and can lead to death, from a social and intellectual evolutionary perspective, there are positive aspects of it as well. Without risky experiences, there would be little impetus for discovery. Risk-taking was obviously adaptive in earlier hominids who set off to explore unknown regions and, in so doing, eventually populated the earth.

In modern society, there are few lands to discover so people take risk to achieve the sensations they seek. According to Zuckerman, people have a basic need for excitement that they will fill one way or another. Based on this and other research, we start to appreciate that risk-taking is not always irrational, and that it is often part of a person's make up; some people simply have to take risks to feel alive.

On the low-risk side, people seek excitement and stimulus from something as benign as horror movies. Even though we know that watching the movie will scare and even upset us, we go anyway because we seek the excitement. I remember going to the movie theater when I was young to see the 1972 horror film "Mark of the Devil," a controversial film set in Austria during the 18th century witch-hunt phenomenon. This movie was supposed to be so gory and scary that they gave the patrons vomit bags as they entered the theater (a great marketing ploy). I was just a little kid at the time so the mere thought of this movie resulted in many a sleepless night. By the way, I have no idea how I got into this R-rated movie at such a young age to begin with. Well, as scared as I was about going to see this vomit-inducing movie, I was *really* excited about going to see it. To me, the risk of being scared to the point of vomiting was outweighed by the excitement I felt at the prospect of actually seeing the blood and gore.

On the high-risk side, sensation-seekers will seek to eliminate their stimulus deficit by making the decision to engage in very risky and even dangerous behaviors. Such was the case with former Idaho U.S. Senator Larry Craig. Yes, *that* Larry Craig, he of the "wide stance" airport bathroom incident. It seems that former Senator Craig has a thing for getting his freak on in public bathrooms. According to the *Washington City Paper*, in 2004, then-U.S. Sen. Larry Craig was accused of engaging in oral sex with another man in the men's room of Washington, D.C.'s Union Station, allegations which the former Senator denied.

According to the paper, an anonymous man claimed that he had spent time with the senator in Union Station's men's rooms. He alleged that he twice tried to engage in a tryst with Craig and, in both instances, the trysts were interrupted when the stalls started filling up. *When the stalls started filling up*?! What!? Combine that risk factor with the security cameras, the filthy conditions of the bathrooms, and the sex act itself, and a picture gets painted of a man who made the decision that engaging in such an activity was worth the risks.

My "Mark of the Devil" movie-going experience was what is referred to as the *peanuts effect*, where, if my risk of going to see the movie and vomiting came to fruition, the result would have been disappointing but not regretful; in other words, no big deal. Former Senator Larry Craig, on the other hand, engaged in an activity where the manifestation of the risks associated with engaging in his activity (humiliation, national scandal, prison, fines, family pain) he found to be seriously regretful.

This raises the question: If, as I propose throughout this book, by acting in our self-interest, we not only make ourselves happy, but also—eventually—our loved ones and the broader community as well, then why did Larry Craig's choice of self-interested actions have a *negative* impact on himself, his family, the state of Idaho, and the U.S. Senate? The reason is because Larry Craig didn't act rationally in his decision-making process. If he had, he would have determined that the potential negative impact of his high-risk choice to have trysts in public bathrooms would be too significant if he got caught and would have decided not to engage in the activity in those questionable locations. The same reasoning applies to a person's decision to engage in vices such as heroin use, for instance.

But what about the CEO who turns to S&M or the thrill-seeker who engages in BASE-jumping? As it turns out, there is a way to help us answer these types of questions about the potential impact of our decisions and whether or not it is rational to engage in them—even if we believe the choices to be in our self-interest. To facilitate a discussion of this topic, I have developed a model which I call **The Pepper Tree** to help people consider the impact of one's actions and the rationality of engaging in them. This will be explored in Chapter Eight: *The Pepper Tree*.

CHAPTER 07
CHOCOLATE PEPPERS

At some point throughout each day, most people get hungry. Hunger is a basic physiological human drive that motivates us to find and ingest the nutrients we need to survive. And when we get hungry, we seek to satisfy that hunger with foods that bring us pleasure—when we have that option, of course. I say "when we have that option" because, let's face it, 15% of the world's population do not have the luxury of *selecting* the type of foods they want to eat; this population of people simply want *any* food to eat. The Food and Agriculture Organization of the United Nations estimates that 925 million people do not have enough to eat. To put that into perspective, that is more people than the populations of the United States, Canada, and the European Union combined. And if we take into consideration the hunger of micronutrient deficiencies—where people may have foods to eat which alleviate their hunger pangs but lack vital nutrients such as iron, zinc, and vitamin A needed for normal growth and development—the number of "hungry" people in the world increases significantly. And when we Americans think about this global plight of the hungry, what do we do? WING BOWL!

In most developed countries people often eat for sport. And in some places—like the United States—we even have eating contests! Yes, eating *contests* where well-nourished people compete to see who can *eat the most food*! And it's gotten to the point where such competitive gastronomic feats of endurance have taken on names such as "The Wing Bowl"—Philadelphia's premier eating contest where a bunch of already-corpulent guys enter a packed (20,000 attendees!) Philadelphia sports arena with all the pageantry of World Wrestling Entertainment (WWE) to compete against each other to see who can eat the most chicken wings. But The Wing Bowl is not alone. There is: Nathan's Famous Hot Dog Eating Contest; Showboat's Fat Tuesday King Cake Eating Contest; Hooters World Wing Eating Championship (a Wing Bowl copycat); Ben's Chili Bowl's World Chili Eating Championship; Smoke's Poutinerie Annual World Poutine Eating Championship (what the hell is *Poutine?*); The Magnify Credit Union World Ice Cream

Eating Championship; Wild Eggs National Pancake Eating Championship; and the Oktoberfest Zinzinnati World Bratwurst-Eating Championship to name but a few. And to top it all off, there is even an eating *league* called Major League Eating (MLE)! Have we bumped our collective heads?!

I can just imagine a starving kid in Thiekthou, Southern Sudan witnessing such wasteful displays of gluttony and thinking: "«نونجم نيعالملا كلت يه»" (translation: *"Are those motherf'ers CRAZY?!"*). For us Westerners, the equivalent would be like watching a reality television show featuring the four richest people in the world—Carlos Slim (the world's richest person), Bill Gates, Amancio Ortega (of Spanish retailer Zara), and Warren Buffett—compete against each other to see who could shred and then burn the most money within five minutes. Everyone witnessing such a ... *wasteful display of gluttony* ... would look at that spectacle and think: *"Are those motherf'ers CRAZY?!"*

To quote the very funny comedian Chris Rock from his 1996 HBO comedy special "Bring the Pain": "We got so much food in America we're *allergic* to food. Allergic to *food*! Hungry people ain't allergic to *shit*. You think anyone in Rwanda's got a f*cking lactose intolerance?!" Very funny, indeed. But the idea behind the joke rings true: In America, we are so prosperous (relatively) that we can eliminate certain foods from our list of food options and still not sweat it. Americans eat because we *can*. Even when we are not motivated to eat by our hunger, we either eat because we *like* a foodstuff that is available to us or because we simply *want* to eat something at that moment.

"Liking" is a measurement of the pleasure we experience when we eat something. For example, I might eat a piece of chocolate cake and realize that I *like* it; it is pleasing to my palate and eating it brings me a measure of pleasure. "Wanting" is a measurement of the intrinsic motivation to acquire and ingest a food, whether driven by hunger or not. For example, while watching a football game I might eat a big bowl of spaghetti which fills my stomach and satisfies my need of hunger. And even though I would be full from eating the spaghetti, I might still *want* a piece of chocolate cake at that moment. Not because I am hungry, but because … I *like* chocolate cake and I just *want* it. A person's *liking* is stable over time (I like chocolate cake today and I will still like chocolate cake 10 years from now), whereas *wanting* tends to be transient (I am in the mood for a piece of chocolate cake right now, but tomorrow I might not be in the mood for it).

Our *want* for a food can be triggered by many factors. The *want* can be triggered because we *like* something—such as chocolate cake—and, because we *like* chocolate cake and are in the mood for something sweet, we *want* the chocolate cake; and the want can also be triggered because we have a desire (not necessarily a physiological *need*) for a particular food based on a characteristic of that food, even though we may not like the food itself. For instance, when I was a kid, I wanted to eat some spinach so that I could become stronger. Not because I *liked* spinach (I *hated* it when I was a kid), but because Popeye the Sailor ate spinach and it turned him into a superhero. It would have been nice if spinach had tasked good *and* provided me with added strength, but that was not the case.

There are, however, food products that—in addition to satisfying the physiological need of hunger—offer the consumer good taste (satisfying the person's 'like') as well as the ancillary benefit of satisfying their 'want.' Take chocolate, for instance. People looooooove chocolate! And their love of chocolate is not a new phenomenon; it can be traced back to the Aztecs and the Mayans, who began drinking a beverage called *chocolatl* at the royal court as early as 600 BC. The drink was reserved for priests, warriors, and nobility, and was associated with fertility and wisdom. Chocolate is made from the seeds of the Theobroma cacao tree, and "Theobroma" is a Greek term meaning '*food of the gods*,' which is what the Aztecs considered the cacao beans to be.

But *why* do people—the Mayans and the ancient Aztecs especially—love chocolate so much? It can't be the raw taste because, until all of the sugar is added to cocoa, raw chocolate is fairly bitter and not very tasty. And just because post-sugar-added chocolate tastes very good (the 'like'), so what? Lots of things taste good, but we don't crave them like we crave chocolate. A primary reason, I believe, is because chocolate consumption gets people *high*—legally.

Euphoria: a feeling of happiness, confidence, or well-being.

Endorphins are brain chemicals known as *neurotransmitters*, which transmit electrical signals within the nervous system. When released, endorphins interact with the opiate receptors in the brain to reduce our perception of pain. Doing so provides us with a feeling similar to drugs such as morphine and codeine—two drugs that provide pain and stress-relief and make the body feel generally good all over. In addition to decreased feelings of pain, the secretion of endorphins leads to feelings of euphoria and enables the release of sex hormones—which are associated with sexual desire. And what do you think is the most popular endorphin-producing food in the world? You guessed it: Chocolate.

There is a substance found in chocolate, phenylethylamine, that researchers believe causes the brain to release dopamine in the pleasure centers of the brain, which peaks during an orgasm. This, some have argued, is why some women find chocolate to be a surrogate for sex. Chocolate also contains a substance called anandamide which activates the same brain receptors as tetrahydrocannabinol (THC), the agent in marijuana that causes a person to feel "high."

The relationship between chocolate and endorphin release likely explains the mellow, happy, euphoric (maybe even horny?) feelings that many people associate with their 'want' for chocolate. Sure, chocolate offers other health benefits, such as antioxidants, a reduced risk of heart disease, and lower blood pressure. But it's likely that most people are unknowingly attracted to chocolate for its endorphin high. This might explain why the average American eats 11 pounds of chocolate per year. That's equivalent to 40 Hershey's chocolate bars annually, or nearly one per month. And the Swiss? They consume 42 pounds of chocolate per-citizen per-year; the most in the world. No wonder Switzerland is so *peaceful*.

Another food that is right up there with chocolate when it comes to endorphin secretion is the *chili pepper*. In the case of chili peppers, the spicier the pepper, the more endorphins are secreted. Sex is also a potent trigger for endorphin release. So the combination of chocolate, chili peppers, and sex could make for one hell of an explosive evening; or so I've been told.

"Quick, Get Some Milk! Get Some Yogurt!"

The combination of chocolate and chili peppers (conveniently sold as chocolate-covered chili peppers) is considered by many to be a great aphrodisiac. An aphrodisiac is a substance that mellows you out, helps get you in the mood, makes you all warm inside, and even gives you energy. I once heard a story about a guy named "Bradley" who tried to exploit these benefits of chocolate peppers but failed miserably.

As the story goes, one evening, Bradley, who was a college sophomore, and his girlfriend were spending a romantic evening together (no doubt after returning from a kegger). Because the evening was "romantic", Bradley did what all guys do when trying to get their romance on: he popped in his favorite porn DVD—something about big asses and the guys who love them—and things started heating up. Earlier in the day, as Bradley was planning for the romantic evening, he prepared a batch of chocolate peppers and placed them in the refrigerator. And when it was game-time, he reached into the fridge, grabbed a couple of the peppers, and started eating them. When he finished the peppers—his tongue burning violently—Bradley drank some Yoo-hoo to ease the pain, and then resumed making out with his girlfriend.

Then it was go-time. The couple undressed, and Bradley eased his way into position so he could "pleasure" his girlfriend. After a few minutes, his girlfriend started experiencing a tingling feeling that quickly turned into a flat-out burning sensation. She pushed Bradley's head away and started screaming.

Bradley was confused and panicked by his girlfriend's screaming. He had no idea what was happening. Then he thought, "The peppers!" He proceeded to explain to his girlfriend how he'd eaten chocolate peppers to give him a Viagra-like sexual boost and that the capsaicin (the stuff that makes peppers hot) must still be on his tongue. His girlfriend screamed, "Is it like eating jalapeno peppers with nachos?!" Bradley replied, "Yeah, I think so." So his girlfriend started screaming, "THEN QUICK, GET SOME MILK! GET SOME YOGURT! GET A

TURKEY BASTER!" (A *turkey baster*? Really? What college student in the history of college students has ever owned a *turkey baster*?)

Anyway, Bradley looked into his refrigerator and luckily found some milk—with an expiration date of '12/16/2000.' Unfortunately, the date of the incident was '2/27/2001.' But Bradley had no choice; his girlfriend was in serious pain. So he used the soured milk which, according to all accounts, came out of the carton like *cottage cheese*.

After the incident, news of the fiasco spread across the campus and whenever someone saw Bradley's girlfriend (whose name was "Beverly"), they would yell, "Hey, what's up, 'Daisy'?" (as in the "Daisy Cottage Cheese" brand). And Bradley? He became a laughing stock.

This is an example of someone (Bradley) trying to satisfy an esteem need (sexual self-respect, respect of his lover and his friends) by making the decision to eat the Viagra-like chocolate peppers. The problem for Bradley—which I will explore further when I discuss *The Pepper Tree*—was that, in making his decision, he neither considered the risks associated with eating the peppers and performing oral sex on his girlfriend nor the negative effect it would have on his girlfriend if things went awry. If he had, assuming he was rational, Bradley would have either not eaten the chocolate peppers or not performed that particular sex act on his girlfriend. So, in the end, his self-interest-based decision did not bring him pleasure, did not satisfy his esteem needs, did not make him happy, definitely did not make his loved one happy ("Daisy"), and did not make society a better place—although it did make it a funnier one!

The point to be made is this: When we experience a physiological need, we will act in our self-interest to satisfy that need with something that we 'like,' something that we happen to 'want' at that moment (assuming we have options), and something that, ultimately, brings us pleasure and makes us happy. In the decision-making process, however, we must assess the potential risks of our decisions and the possible consequences of our choices. By failing to do so, our acts of "self-interest" become acts of "selfishness," which could, in the end, have a negative impact on ourselves (Bradley, the girlfriendless laughing stock), our loved ones (Beverly/Daisy), and the broader community.

CHAPTER

THE PEPPER TREE

08

A DECISION-SUPPORT TOOL

The Pepper Tree Decision-Support Tool ("The Pepper Tree") is my version of a decision tree, only useful. A decision tree is a decision-making model that works on an "if-then" basis where each possible outcome of a decision presents a number of different options, or "branches," that the decision-maker can follow next. The thinking behind the decision tree process is that when the decision-maker has chosen all of his or her courses of action—which are themselves based on a preceding course of action—he or she will have arrived at a well-considered decision.

When I was in business school, we had a riddle that we would ask of incoming first-year MBA candidates who were about to get their first exposure to decision trees. We would present the riddle in the same manner in which former "Tonight Show" television host Johnny Carson would deliver his *Carnac the Magnificent* routine, where he would give the answers to an unknown question first and *then* read the question as the punchline. We would say: Training wheels, teething rings, decision trees: Name three things that you will never use again in life.

The Pepper Tree, unlike a decision tree, is practically-useful, focused, based on the user's experience and opinion, and guides the user down a path toward making (or deciding not to make) a decision that is in the user's self-interest. It's an easy-to-use 'If-Then-Why' tool that can supplement the decision-making process, helping to determine whether to engage in an activity or not based on its likely impact on the decision-maker and on society as a whole. As a result, it will increase the odds that a decision will lead to a pleasurable outcome. The tool compels its user to ask: 'If' I decide to engage in a certain activity 'then' what are the potential outcomes of that decision? And based on the likely outcomes of the decision action, 'why' should I consider engaging in that activity?

The Pepper Tree helps ensure that when its user makes a decision about the best course of action for satisfying a need, the decision is not only made in their self-interest, but is also made after considering the following: the expected utility (the *value*) of the action; the risks associated with the decision options; the possible consequences if the risks materialize; the impact of the decision's outcome on others; the degree to which the decision will provide pleasure and satisfy the need; the expected degree of happiness to be derived from their decision action; and the attractiveness of engaging in the activity that results from the decision.

THE PEPPER TREE

The Pepper Tree Decision-Support Tool forces the decision-maker to consider the expected outcomes, the likelihood of making a satisfaction-decision, and the implications of choosing between the various courses of action that the decision-maker is confronted with. The tool consists of a work chart with ten categories, each with a corresponding rating scale that ranges from '10' (good) to '0' (not so good). The tool encourages the decision-maker (the tool's user or subject) to develop an honest assessment of whether or not a decision action (the activity that will be engaged in based on the decision that is made) will result in a desired outcome and, consequently, whether or not the action is in the decision-maker's self-interest and therefore "worth" engaging in.

The **Pepper Tree Work Chart**—a decision-support worksheet of sorts—is provided to help the user assess the expected benefits, risks, and implications of a decision. The Pepper Tree Work Chart is provided below, and a full-size version of the chart can be downloaded from the website: www.ChocolatePeppers.com. It consists of the following ten elements that I believe people should consider as they make decisions about whether or not to engage in an activity:

- Why consider taking an action? Need vs. Want
- The type of need being addressed
- The relative value of the options/choices available to satisfy the need

- The impact of the options for satisfying a primary need on a higher-level need
- The subject's experience with the available options
- The amount of pleasure expected to be received from the decision action
- The risks associated with the available options
- Happiness impact: the degree of happiness expected to be derived from the decision action
- The impact of the decision on others
- The overall attractiveness of engaging in the decision action (go/no-go)

Each element of The Pepper Tree Work Chart is explained in greater detail below.

CHOCOLATE PEPPERS

THE PEPPER TREE WORK CHART

The Consideration — Score

Why Consider	Need Type	Value of the Choice	Impact on Higher Need	Experience	Pleasure Amount	Risk Level	Happiness Impact	Impact on Others	TOTAL SCORE
		High	Low	Lots	High	Low	Positive	Positive	Consider
Need	**Basic** Food Shelter Water Sleep Oxygen								
10		10	10	10	10	10	10	10	80
9		9	9	9	9	9	9	9	72
8	**Safety** Security Stability Order Physical Safety	8	8	8	8	8	8	8	64
7		7	7	7	7	7	7	7	56
6		6	6	6	6	6	6	6	48
5		5	5	5	5	5	5	5	40
4	**Love** Affection Identification Companionship	4	4	4	4	4	4	4	32
3	**Esteem** Self-respect Prestige Success Respect	3	3	3	3	3	3	3	24
2		2	2	2	2	2	2	2	16
1		1	1	1	1	1	1	1	8
0	**Actualize** Self-fulfillment Understanding Achievement	0	0	0	0	0	0	0	0
Want		Low	High	None	Low	High	Negative	Negative	Re-consider

2012 Tab Edwards

The Pepper Tree Work Chart Elements

Why consider taking an action?
Need vs. Want

A "need" is a requirement or a necessity for functionality or performance. For instance, in order for a gas-engine car to run, it *needs* gasoline. In order for a person to survive in the desert, she *needs* water. In order for children to build strong bones and teeth, they *need* calcium. In order for former National Basketball Association (NBA) player Latrell Sprewell to feed his family, he *needs* $7 million per year—or so he said when he turned down a 3-year, $21 million dollar contract offer from the Minnesota Timberwolves. Okay, so maybe Latrell's family budget is a bad example of a genuine need, but you get the idea.

A "want," on the other hand, is what I call a *luxury*. A want is a desire that people experience even when we are *satiated*. Satiation works something like this: When we are hungry, for example, we will begin to eat food to satisfy that hunger. When the food enters our gastronomical tract (digestive system), it is digested and absorbed and signals are sent to the brain indicating that food is being absorbed and the body is starting to feel better. This induces satiation which urges us to stop eating. So, if we continue to *want* food even after a state of satiation has been achieved (where our hunger is satisfied so we don't *need* to eat anymore), then we are no longer acting toward the satisfaction of a basic need (that has already been accomplished), but are, instead, exercising the luxury of eating just for the hell of it.

Take the situation of two men: one a starving South Asian man who hasn't eaten anything for an entire week, and the other is 340-pound champion sumo wrestler Hakuho Sho who eats 20,000 calories daily (the equivalent of thirteen large cheese pizzas each day). Sitting on a table in front of the two men is a cheese sandwich. Which of the two men would "need" that sandwich? Which of the two men would only "want" that sandwich? The South Asian man would *need* the sandwich to keep him alive, and Hakuho would simply *want* the sandwich out of habit.

I also say that "want" is a luxury because, even if we have a genuine physiological need for food, some people have the luxury of *deciding* on and choosing the foods they want to eat in order to satisfy their hunger. If a person is hungry he might "want" Lobster Florentine to eat, but our bodies might only "need" horsebread to satisfy the hunger. In this example, Lobster Florentine is a want, a luxury, whereas horsebread or ANY food is a need.

When I purchased that $5,000 suit, did I *need* the suit? No. But I damn sure *wanted* it. And that's not a bad thing.

In this *Why consider taking an action* category of The Pepper Tree Work Chart, the importance rating scale ranges from '10' to '0.' If the reason why the user is considering taking an action is based on genuine *need*, then the user would score the activity based on their opinion of the genuineness of the need. For example, the cheese sandwich for the starving South Asian man would score a '10' on the rating scale because he truly has a genuine hunger need; the more genuine the need, the higher the score. And if the user is satiated and is considering taking an action based on the user's *want* for something, the user should score the consideration low (e.g. the cheese sandwich for sumo wrestler Hakuho would score a '1' on the rating scale).

The type of need being addressed

The basic need that is motivating the subject to take an action

As I wrote in Chapter Three: *"Why Did I Buy That Suit?"* all human behavior is aimed toward the satisfaction of basic human needs. Psychologist Abraham Maslow (he of "A Theory of Human Motivation" fame) believed that the following needs are similar to instincts and play a major role in motivating behavior:

Maslow's Hierarchy of Needs

	Deficiency Needs ("D" Needs)				Being Needs ("B" Needs)
Physiological Needs	Safety Needs	Love Needs	Esteem Needs		Self-Actualization Needs
- Food - Shelter - Water - Sleep - Oxygen	- Security - Order - Stability - Physical Safety	- Affection - Identification - Companionship	- Self-respect - Prestige - Success - Respect of Others		- Self-fulfillment - Understanding - Achieving ones own potential

▲ Primary Needs ▲ Higher-Level Needs

There is no rating scale in the *Type of Need* category of The Pepper Tree Work Chart. The user should select the type of need which he or she believes is motivating the consideration or behavior. This will serve as the foundation for the seven remaining categories of The Pepper Tree Work Chart.

The relative value of the options/ choices available to satisfy the need

When it comes to satisfying needs, many people are fortunate to have a number of options available to them that will satisfy those needs. You hungry? Go get a cheese sandwich. You thirsty? Go get a beer. You need security? Go buy a gun. You need affection? Go get a hooker. You need self-esteem? Then stop eating cheese sandwiches, drinking beer, playing with guns, and buying hookers!

The various options available to us as we pursue the satisfaction of a need can vary in their *value* or overall benefit. Imagine you were lost in the middle of the Sahara Desert for a week—where the daily temperature reaches 136 degrees Fahrenheit—and you were literally dying of thirst. Once you were found, the options available to you were: a cold bottle of spring water, a hot cup of coffee, and a glass of vodka. Which of the three options would have the highest value to you? In this scenario, the bottle of water would be of higher value than either the coffee or the vodka. The first reason is because water is a vital nutrient; we cannot survive without water. The second reason is because the only value in the other two drinks is their water content. The third reason is because the temperature is 136 degrees in the Sahara Desert, and who the hell would want to drink HOT coffee or *anything* with the nickname "Fire Water" when it's 136 degrees outside?!

As I wrote earlier, sometimes people make decisions for which there is no logical basis (eating crème brulee). But such decisions are not necessarily bad decisions, they might just not be the best or most rational decisions. If you emerged from the Sahara Desert and, instead of choosing the bottle of cold water, you chose the cup of hot coffee, that wouldn't be the most rational choice, but, because your body would absorb the water content in the coffee, it would still help revive you. So while this decision is not the most *rational* decision, it's not necessarily a *bad* decision.

The same applies to food. Let's say, after eating a bunch of chocolate peppers one day, you realized that you had the munchies; this is because the anandamide that is contained in chocolate activates the same brain receptors as THC—the stuff in marijuana. In order to satisfy the munchies (hunger), you go to the refrigerator looking for something to eat. When you open the door, you're greeted by a wide variety of edible options: fruit, vegetables, fish, ice cream, donuts, cookies, and pigs' feet; you choose the cookies. Rationally, the fruit, vegetables, and fish would provide your hungry body with the most nutritional value. So on The Pepper Tree rating scale, these items would be rated higher than the cookies would be. But don't forget: just because your choice may not be the most rational or, in this case, the most nutritional, it could still be considered a good choice. Why? Because the cookies will bring you pleasure which will make you happy, and your good mood will ultimately benefit others.

A quick note about "value." What exactly is *value*? Value is a term that is used frequently but is tough to define. In the simplest sense, *value* is like beauty: it is in the mind of the receiver. A quick way to help you understand the concept of value and to determine the value of the object in question, is to ask yourself the following: Imagine what your life would be like without [the object]? What if [the object] didn't exist? Now imagine your life with [the object]. The difference between your life without [the object] and your life with [the object] is the value that [the object] provides you. What if [the object] was *cookies*? What if [the object] was *water*. Which is more valuable to you?

Psychologists Daniel Kahneman and Amos Tversky argued that the *carriers* of value are changes in wealth or welfare, rather than the final states of wealth and welfare. They go on to argue that value should be treated as a function in two arguments: a reference point and the magnitude of the positive or negative change from that reference point. Simplistically: The greater the change in one's wealth or welfare, the greater the value and thus, the greater the value of [the object] that caused the change. This is consistent with my position on value: If you were lost in the Sahara Desert, the cold bottle of spring water would result in a far more dramatic—and positive—change in your condition (welfare) than the glass of vodka. Therefore, in an *absolute* sense, the water would hold the most value for you. I stress "in an *absolute* sense" because, let's face it, in a *relative* sense an alcoholic might consider the vodka to be of more value to him.

Absolutism means that some things are cast-in-stone and agreed on by all *normal* people. For example, if you stick your hand in fire, it will burn and hurt, regardless of the situation. In this example, fire burning and hurting a person's hand is an absolute; it's gonna happen in all cases. *Relativism*, on the other hand, acknowledges that, given the context of the situation, ideas that you think are absolute may not be absolute. For example, a 300-pound woman, by today's standard, is considered "fat." But in a world where everyone weighs 1,200 pounds, the 300-pound woman is Lolo Jones. In this relative sense, a 300-pound woman is not fat, so 300 pounds is not fat in an *absolute* sense. Have you ever heard the saying: "In the land of the blind, the one-eyed man is king"? Same thing: Relative.

In The Pepper Tree Work Chart, this category has a rating scale of '10' (High value) to '0' (Low value). In the previous example of the Sahara Desert, the bottle of cold water would have a very high value ('10') and the glass of vodka would have a low value. This is because water, more than coffee, vodka, or any other beverage, satisfies our *thirst* need most effectively and humans need water to survive. So its value to humans is of the highest rating.

The impact of the options for satisfying a primary need on a higher-level need

This category asks the user to consider the impact that the satisfaction of a Primary Need might have on a Higher-level Need. This category has a *reverse* rating scale. If a need is rated as a '10' on *this* scale, it means that the Primary Need will have *no* negative impact on a Higher-Level Need. Conversely, if the Primary Need is rated as a '0' on this scale, it means that engaging in the activity *will* have a negative impact on the satisfaction of a Higher-Level Need. For example, if you are the starving South Asian man, then eating the cheese sandwich (the Primary Need for "food") resolves a genuine physiological need and will not negatively impact a Higher-level Need; that's a good thing. And because it is good, it should be rated as a '10' on the rating scale.

If, however, the user was an obese, 750-pound man with heart trouble, resolving his hunger need by eating that cheese sandwich could negatively impact his ability to satisfy a safety need (health), a love need (finding companionship), an esteem need (self-respect and the respect of others), and even an Actualization Need (achieving his fullest potential). In the obese man's case, satisfying his Primary Need with the cheese sandwich should be rated very low— possibly even a '0'—because of the negative impact it could have on a Higher-Level Need.

The subject's experience with the chosen options

When presented with options, a person will choose among the options based on the pleasure and satisfaction the person expects to receive from the chosen option. *Satisfaction* relates to the degree of fulfillment one receives from a decision, whether it is a purchase decision, a relationship decision, or some other action or engagement in an activity. Satisfaction is a function of *expectation*. It is a function of some initial standard and one's perceived discrepancy from that initial standard. If there is alignment between an option's expected performance (functioning, usefulness, production, utility, or pleasure contribution) and the option's actual performance, then the option will provide satisfaction.

When I was in high school I read the book *The Hobbit* by J.R.R. Tolkien, and I enjoyed the book very much. Some years later, the book was made into a feature film, and I was excited to see it because I had enjoyed the book so much. As a result, my expectations for the movie were very high. I went to see the movie and, after what felt like eight hours, I woke up to find it was just ending. I *hated* that movie! It was long and *boring*! I realize that my opinion is probably in the minority, but so what? It's *my* opinion, and to me, *my* opinion of the movie's likability is the one that counts. My *expected* level of enjoyment of the film was not matched by my actual perceived enjoyment of the film, so there was a discrepancy between the two. That discrepancy resulted in the dissatisfaction of my ticket purchase.

When the sequel to the film was released, my expected level of enjoyment of the sequel was low—based on my prior experience with the original Hobbit movie—so I avoided seeing the sequel. This is the value of experience. My expectations for the original film, my decision to see the film based on these high expectations, and my post-decision evaluation of the film after having seen it affected my future decision of whether to see the sequel or not. My experience with the original film informed my future decision to skip the sequel and avoid potential displeasure.

People make decisions that offer a positive payoff, that provide us with pleasure. We *learn* which decisions to make, which activities to engage in and which activities to avoid. These decisions are based on our experience of having received either pleasure and satisfaction or displeasure as a result of an action. This learning process (experiences providing us with memories that result in learning) helps us to make better decisions which result in more pleasurable (and safer) choices. This makes us happier overall and more fulfilled and helps us to survive as a species. And as we gain experience with and learn from the activities we engage in and the choices we make, we increase our odds of making better decisions down the road, thus enabling us to better answer the important question: How do we know that a decision will result in a desired outcome?

This category of The Pepper Tree Work Chart (*The subject's experience with the satisfaction options*) has a rating scale of '10' (the user has lots of experience with a decision choice) to '0' (the user has no experience with the decision choice). The logic behind this category says that we will make better, more informed, and more pleasurable decisions about things in which we have prior experience. For that reason, having "lots" of experience would get a rating of '10' on the rating scale. Conversely, if a person has no experience with a particular decision or option, the payoff and pleasure quotient are personally unknown, so the expectation of pleasure or satisfaction from a decision is also unknown, which means that the highest score such an option should receive is between a '0' and a '5' (neutral).

The amount of pleasure expected to be received from the decision action

This is directly related to *The Subject's Experience with the Satisfaction Options*. If the tool's user has no experience with a particular decision action or selected option, the degree of satisfaction the user can expect to receive is unknown; this could result in the user making an ill-advised or bad decision. However, if the user has extensive experience with a decision action or selected option and the experience was a pleasurable and satisfying one, the user will have greater confidence that engaging in that particular activity will result in a positive outcome, and will therefore make a better decision.

Reference experience is also useful in helping people who have no direct, personal experience make a decision based on an expectation of pleasure that would likely be received from the decision action. Reference experience is like second-hand experience: you haven't experienced the activity *yourself*, but you have witnessed other people engage in the activity and, based on the outcome of their experience with the activity, are provided with insight that will help you make a more informed decision about that activity.

But something puzzles me: In the year 2013 and, with the benefit of reference experience, why are there *new* crack-heads joining the ranks?! I don't understand it! Who, tell me *who*, is the person who says, "Hmm, that 98-pound smoker who just asked me for a quarter lives under a bridge, smells like piss, has no teeth, has grey skin, and walks around scratching his balls. Yes! I want to be like *him*!" Who *says* that?! Who?! How is it humanly possible that in today's day and age, people still make the decision to smoke crack? I guess it's just one of life's eternal mysteries.

This category of The Pepper Tree Work Chart has a rating scale of '10' (the user has experience with the option and expects to receive a "High" amount of pleasure from the decision action) to '0' (the user has experience with the option and expects to receive a "Low" amount of pleasure from the decision action, or the user has no experience with the decision choice and has no experiential basis for an expectation of pleasure). I *love* vanilla Oreo cookies, and when I make the decision to purchase them, I know from experience that I will receive maximum pleasure from eating them. But I have never eaten hog head cheese (and based on the looks of it, I have zero desire to do so), so the amount of pleasure I could expect to receive from making the decision to eat it would be scored low-to-neutral at best.

The risks associated with the available options

There is a notion in business, investing, and gambling that the greater the risk, the greater the return. I'm not so sure, however, that this also applies to non-material decisions. I wrote earlier that humans have a stimulus deficit, which we try to eliminate by seeking stimulation from risky and dangerous activities. In some cases, the greater the perceived risk of an activity, the greater the stimulation (excitement) reward—assuming you survive the activity. Riding roller coasters is exciting because of the perceived risk of going high in the air, moving fast around sharp curves, and the (remote) possibility of flying out of your seat. The same is true for bungee jumping: because of the perceived risks, it's scary, but if you survive it, the adrenaline rush makes the post-landing experience wildly fun and exhilarating.

So if riding a *roller coaster* is fun because of the stimulation (excitement) received due to the perceived (minimal) risk of the activity, imagine what the excitement level must be of engaging in a high-risk activity like free-solo climbing. Free-solo climbing is an activity in which its daredevil practitioners climb dangerous mountains alone, without ropes or any other technical equipment. Typically, their only gear consists of rubber-soled shoes, pants, a shirt, and chalk to dry the sweat from their hands—hands they use to pull themselves up the sides of mountains. If you have ever seen video footage of free-solo climbers in action, you can confirm that it is scary to even *watch*!

In 1993, 36-year-old free-solo climber Derek Geoffrey Hersey was killed when he fell while climbing Yosemite National Park's Sentinel Rock. In Hersey's case, the risk came to fruition. But does the risk and inherent danger of free-solo climbing mean he should not have engaged in the sport? In hindsight, most people would argue that he should not have engaged in it because the activity is very risky and dangerous, and it resulted in his unfortunate death. But what if free-solo climbing compensated for his stimulus deficit and provided him with pleasure, excitement, and happiness? If so, then I believe that he *should* have engaged in the sport because his happiness and fulfillment while living likely made him a better person, which positively impacted the lives of everyone around him.

For some people, the risk-related fear induced by the potential danger of an activity is the carrier of value for the risk-taker. BASE (Buildings, Antennas, Spans, and Earth)-jumping is a dangerous sport in which its practitioners illegally climb onto buildings, mountains or other base platforms and then jump. When the jumper approaches the ground, he or she then opens their parachute in hopes of a safe landing. Why do they do it? Why do BASE-jumpers engage in such a dangerous practice? Russian BASE-jumper Valery Rozov—one of the premier

BASE-jumpers and sky-divers in the world—says that it's the excitement: "The conditions of the jumps are usually unpredictable so this means that before every jump you are nervous. Even though I have done thousands of jumps I get scared a little bit. But it's exciting ..."

Looking at the examples of free-solo climbing and BASE-jumping, it becomes evident that the practitioners clearly understand the known and potentially fatal risks associated with performing the sports, and they still make the informed, *experience-based* decision to participate in them. But, for these athletes, the expected payoff or gains they receive (the satisfaction that comes from successfully completing the climb or jump—i.e. "surviving") must loom larger than the expected losses. I'm sure that none of the practitioners *actually* think they are going to die during their next jump or climb, otherwise they would be biased toward maintaining the status-quo by not climbing or jumping. But because they climb and jump, they are better people and the world is a better place.

I can hear the questions now: "So let me get this straight: It's okay for a free-solo climber to accept the potentially-deadly risks associated with climbing and, because he or she does, the world is somehow a better place for it. But what about the person who knowingly accepts the risks associated with smoking crack, shooting heroin, or smoking crystal meth? Are *they* helping to make the world a better place, too?" That's a fair question, and there are a couple of ways it can be addressed: quizzically or straightforwardly. First, quizzically.

Over the years, Civil Libertarians (people who believe in the supremacy of individual rights and personal freedoms over any kind of authority) have argued that there should not be laws against drug use and that people who use drugs should be allowed to do so at their own risk and without threat of criminal prosecution. Following this argument, heroin addicts should be allowed to shoot as much heroin into their veins as they can afford. And if they happen to die of a heroin overdose? Oh well. That's the consequence of your free-will-based decision.

People who support these forms of civil liberties believe, as in this example, that heroin addicts—or those addicted to other dangerous drugs—will consume the amount of the drug they need to keep themselves feeling "good" and not sick. And, eventually, they will all die of drug overdoses or other illnesses and, in 100 years, there will be fewer, if any, serious drug addicts remaining in the world. So, in the end, drug addicts who make the conscious decision to assume the risk of using dangerous drugs will gain some measure of pleasure from their actions (drug fix), which will make them happy and less belligerent, and then they will eventually overdose and die off. And when they do, the world will be a better place. So, the cynics will argue, my model of self-interested behavior (drug abuse) leading to the betterment of the world (the extinction of drug addicts) even holds true when the decision-maker acts in his or her self-interest and makes the decision to engage in known-hazardous activities.

Now, straightforwardly. As you will see when I provide some examples of how the use of The Pepper Tree Work Chart helps with the decision-making process, drug addicts would have to make the decision of whether or not to smoke crack or shoot heroin after considering the risks of engaging in the activity and the potential impact of their actions on other people. However—and this is important—as I outlined previously in my Rational Routing Routine (R3) decision-making model, when people make decisions, three conditions must be met in order for the decision-maker to make a "good" decision:

1. **Rationality**: This assumes that people are basically mentally sane and they exercise sound judgment and use common sense when making decisions. It is debatable whether or not a heroin or crack addict is acting rationally or, depending on how far gone they are, if they are still mentally sane. According to The National Institute on Drug Abuse, drug addiction is a mental illness. Drug addiction affects the addict's brain, disrupting their normal hierarchy of needs and making the procurement and use of their drug of choice the priority need. This weakens their ability to control impulses, *despite the negative consequences*, similar to characteristics of other mental illnesses.

2. **Logic**: A person's thought process should follow a logical course. It is debatable whether or not a drug addict is thinking logically when they need a fix.

3. **Cause-and-effect considerations**: When addiction

takes hold of a person, I do not believe the addict is carefully considering that if he or she shoots too much heroin, they could die.

Given the evidence, I do not believe that drug addicts think rationally when making the decision to abuse drugs and, therefore, should be excluded from consideration in the proposal that a person acting in his or her self-interest achieves pleasure and happiness, ultimately resulting in the betterment of society.

And suicide? Same thing.

What about laws? One may argue that when we obey laws, we are not acting in our own self-interest or of our own free will, but are, instead, being affected by an external influence (the law). Laws are guidelines which are defined and enforced to govern behavior. They are designed to prevent (as much as possible) chaos. And when we break the law, there are consequences. Even though we may disagree with certain laws, we all agree that laws are necessary. That said, there are a few questionable ones on the books, such as those that make the following things illegal: spitting in public, sleeping on top of a refrigerator outdoors, and becoming Governor if the candidate has participated in a duel.

But even though laws exist that discourage certain behaviors (such as selling automobiles on Sunday), people still have the option of obeying or disobeying a law. When we do so, however, we must take the potential risk (penalty, in this case) into consideration. Should I run that red light? I will weigh the pros and cons of running the light before making that split-second decision: If I'm running late for an important job interview and I run the red light, I will arrive at my destination on time and that will help my job prospects. If I run the red light, there is a chance I will not be caught by the police. If I run the red light and get caught by the police, I will either be let go with a warning or I will be given a traffic ticket. But either way, it will take lots of time to go through the motions. If I run the red light I might get into a car accident, and that would suck! Ultimately, I might decide that running the red light offers the best payoff because the prospect of being on time and getting that new job far outweighs the low risk of getting caught running the light. In this case, I would act in my self-interest, assume the risk, run the red light, and arrive at the job interview on time. And when I do, I would be happy that I made the decision. And because I would be happy, I would probably have a good interview, and the good interview would increase my chances of getting the job.

Whether it is free-solo climbing, running red lights, shooting heroin, drinking alcohol excessively, smoking cigarettes, or eating a cheese sandwich, people make rational decisions after considering the risks associated with their decision options as well as the expected payoff, utility, or level of satisfaction brought by the decision. And, if we are rational and consider the elements of The Pepper Tree, the decision that we ultimately make will be in our self-interest.

In The Pepper Tree Work Chart, this *Risks* category has a reverse rating scale of '10' ("Low" risk option) to '0' ("High" risk option). In the previous example of running the red light, the risk of running the light (getting a traffic ticket, getting into a car accident—a *medium* risk with a rating of '5' on the scale) was outweighed by the expected payoff of arriving at the job interview on time.

Happiness Impact:
The degree of happiness expected
to be derived from the decision action

When acting in our self-interest and free from external influence, we attribute value to an action because it satisfies a need within us and the satisfaction of our needs brings us personal satisfaction which contributes to our general happiness. If you were free to do absolutely *anything* without having to think about any external influences—"If I buy these golf clubs, my wife will be *pissed*!"; "If I go to the mall without my spoiled, bratty kids, they will be disappointed"; "If I wear my Sly Stone silver platform Disco boots, the neighbors will think I'm *crazy*"; "Although I really want to hook up with that sloppy fat guy loser who doesn't have a job, if I do, my girlfriends will ridicule me"—you would likely act in your own self-interest, say "Screw them!", and do the thing that makes you feel good.

Human beings are pleasure-seekers and every opportunity we have to do so, we will act in a way that not only satisfies a need but also brings us satisfaction. And we give the highest priority to those actions that bring us the *most* pleasure, satisfaction, and happiness. If you could take a job paying $10 per hour or the exact same job paying $15 per hour, you would choose the $15 per hour job. If you could drive around in a 2014 Porsche 911 Cabriolet automobile or a 1977 AMC Pacer, you would drive the Porsche. If you could eat chitterlings or chateaubriand steak, you would eat the steak. And, ladies, if you could date "Sexiest Man Alive" actor Channing Tatum or Paul "Pee-Wee Herman" Reubens, you would date Channing Tatum.

Everyone will agree that if you were broke and down-on-your-luck, you would love having that $10 per hour job; if you were a slave to the public transportation system, you would appreciate that 1977 Pacer; if you were lonely and stranded on a deserted island with no prospect of finding a man, Pee-Wee Herman just might suffice; and if you were lost in the wilderness for an entire week with absolutely nothing to eat, you would welcome that bowl of chitterlings. On second thought, scratch that; there's no way in hell I'm eating chitterlings!

The point is that when we can act of our own free will, unencumbered by external influence, we will make self-interested choices based on the expected payoff of those choices. And when choosing between alternatives—all things being equal—we will choose the option that brings us the most pleasure and makes us happiest, and we will eschew the options that bring us little-to-no pleasure or satisfaction.

In The Pepper Tree Work Chart, this *Happiness impact* category has a rating scale of '10' ("Positive" impact) to '0' ("Negative" impact), with a rating of '5' indicating "neutral" or no impact. If I was in a satiated state (relatively content with no real physiological need to satisfy) and I had to make a decision about eating chitterlings, I would rate them a '0' on this rating scale, because simply *smelling* the chitterlings would literally make me vomit, so I can only imagine what *eating them* would do to me. And if eating chitterlings was rated a '0' on my happiness scale, I would be inclined to not engage in the activity.

The impact of the decision on others

Unless you are a space alien who has been plopped down here on earth with no family, relatives, or other personal relationships, nearly every decision that you make will impact or affect someone else in one way or another. Fred decides to go out drinking with his friends and consumes 15 shots of whiskey; he gets plastered. He then decides to drive home — 45 minutes away — with his friends in the passenger seats. He misjudges a turn and crashes into another vehicle. Fred's decision to drive while drunk not only impacted himself, but also his friends, the passengers in the other vehicle, the police department, the fire department, his family (Fred would most certainly have to pay more money for his automobile insurance), and the other uninvolved motorists whose travel times will be slowed as a result of the accident.

In this example, Fred's decision to drive while drunk had a negative impact on many people. And if Fred had acted rationally *before* he started drinking (acknowledging the likelihood of getting really drunk after drinking 15 shots of whiskey) he would have made contingency transportation arrangements that would have been in everyone's best interest. The decision action of drinking the 15 shots of whiskey was not the problem—well, at least not *this* problem—but his decision to *drive* after drinking the whiskey was ultimately the most ill-advised one.

This is a rather obvious example of how one's actions can have a negative and injurious impact on other people. But our decisions can impact others in more subtle, yet no less harmful, ways. Suppose, for instance, that superstar professional basketball player LeBron James announced in an interview being aired during the National Football League Super Bowl game—an event viewed by 108 million people in the United States alone—that the reason he performs so well on the basketball court is because, before each game, he sneaks off to the bathroom to smoke—and inhale—two hand-rolled Cuban cigars. Hundreds of thousands, if not millions, of kids around the world who look up to LeBron James as a role model and superhero would start smoking cigars in hopes of improving their sports performance or to simply "be like LeBron." The result would be an exponential increase in the number of lung cancer incidents worldwide. This would negatively impact these new smokers' families, communities, and even social services. So while, on the surface, LeBron's (hypothetical) pre-game ritual would seem to only harm LeBron, his action would also indirectly impact communities around the world. And once the ill-effects of the carcinogens began to negatively affect LeBron's basketball performance, his loved ones, his basketball team, and the entire National Basketball Association would also be hurt.

This fictitious LeBron James story is not just an example of how one athlete's actions can negatively impact his basketball team, but also how one member of any team—business, support group—can hurt the team and its performance by their inconsiderate and selfish (not *self-interested*) actions. But just because a decision action you decide to engage in may have a negative impact on others, does that mean you shouldn't engage in the activity? I say, no. I am a proponent of doing whatever the hell you want to do. However, I also believe that when we make decisions to engage in certain activities, we subconsciously take into consideration what I call the emotional "invisible ball & chain." When we engage in behaviors that violate our personal beliefs or values, even though we might not feel bad about the act at the time we commit it, and even if we could be assured that no one would know about our performance of the act, we would still be plagued by an internally bad feeling—like carrying around a ball & chain—until we did something to clear our conscience.

Imagine that you could do absolutely anything that you wanted to do without anyone ever knowing about it. You would be free to engage in any activity that you could imagine, without the risk of public disapproval, punishment, legal action, or retribution. If that was the case, then what would you do? Would you sneak into a movie theater? Would you hack into someone's computer system? Would you look at someone's confidential data at work? Would you beat up your neighborhood's bully? Would you pimp-slap your enemy? Men: would you lurk in a women's locker room? Women: would you hang out in a men's locker room—with a video camera? Would you steal something needlessly? Think about it for a moment: You are omnipotent and can do absolutely *anything* without anyone ever knowing about it *and* you would still be admitted into your version of the hereafter. Would you do *any* of these things? With the possible exception of sneaking into a movie theater, pimp-slapping your enemy, and beating up your neighborhood's bully, I am willing to bet that most people would not. But why? A major reason why people do not engage in activities that they may truly want to engage in is because of reputation (what other people will think about them), fear of punishment, fear of reprisal, or fear of religious damnation. But even if these outcomes were guaranteed not to occur, people would still not do certain things. The reason: *Remorse*.

Remorse is an emotional feeling of personal regret that a rational person experiences after he or she has committed an act which the person believes—for various reasons—to be a violation of a highly-held personal belief, a social norm, or a law. Remorse is closely linked to *guilt*. A person who experiences remorse will never be truly fulfilled because their remorseful act will inhibit their achievement of *self-respect*, and if their remorseful action becomes known, the *respect of others* as well—both of which are esteem needs. And, based on Maslow's Hierarchy of Needs, a person cannot be *totally* fulfilled (not just merely fulfilled) if the person is unable to achieve *self-actualization*—a state that is impossible to reach without satisfying one's esteem needs.

A *psychopath* is, by definition, a person who is irrational and has a flagrant disregard for societal rules and norms. Therefore, they feel no remorse or misgivings about committing an act that is generally considered to be a violation of a social custom or a law. Serial killers are considered psychopaths because they have neither regard for the law nor any feeling of guilt about their heinous murderous actions.

Assuming that a person is not psychopathic, they would feel a sense of remorse and guilt when violating a personal belief, rule, or law—even if no one else in the world knew about the person's violation. If a rational person hit someone with his car on a deserted road in the middle of an Iowa cornfield at 3AM, he would feel terrible about it, even if no one would ever find about the hit-and-run. In this example, the person would feel terrible because he would be remorseful about having violated a personally-held belief (that we shouldn't harm innocent people), a social more (if we do something bad, we should confess to it), or a law (hit-and-run, and leaving the scene of a crime). We often hear about cases where someone commits a serious crime and then voluntarily turns themselves in to the police because the feelings of remorse and guilt they were experiencing had become so overwhelming they could no longer operate "normally." So even if it was guaranteed that no one would ever know about the hit-and-run, the driver would still know what he did and would feel a bothersome sense of inner-guilt and remorse—the *invisible ball & chain*. And these nagging feelings create stress which will affect the person's health (contributing to problems such as high blood pressure, heart disease, obesity, and diabetes), even though he might not realize it. This is an example of how a person's actions can impact the victim, social services, and the person himself.

This raises a question worth exploring: What about people who keep secrets which, if known by another party, would negatively impact the other party? But if the secret information was *not* shared, it would not have an impact on the other party. Is that a bad thing? My answer to that question is: maybe, maybe not. Take marital infidelity, for example.

A Gallup poll found that 92% of people polled believe that having an extramarital affair is morally wrong. However, other polls show that anywhere between 20% and 70% of married people engage in extramarital affairs. This would imply that, although we *say* that we believe having an affair is "wrong," we don't really mean it. And if that's the case, then having an affair would appear to be an activity that most people engage in and feel that—as long as their spouse or partner doesn't know about it— it's okay. But that would mean that if we act in our self-interest and decide to engage in an affair, most of us would not experience much in the way of remorse and would simply consider it a need-satisfying activity that provides us with pleasure, satisfies us sexually and emotionally, and makes us happy—even if only in the short-term.

I don't want to sound as if I'm endorsing infidelity, but if I am to be consistent in my belief that acting in our self-interest is a good thing, then I cannot suddenly say that people should not engage in infidelity just because external influences (92% of people believing it to be immoral) tell us it is wrong. The consenting adults who decide to engage in the activity have to make that determination based on their situation and circumstance. And if these adults make the decision rationally—taking into consideration the elements of The Pepper Tree model, especially *risk* and the *impact on others*—and the decision still proves to be a good one, they should go for it.

But having an affair is not simply a matter of a married man or woman doin' the stick-n-move with another person; it is more complex than that. According to psychologist Douglas LaBier, who has studied marital affairs for more than a decade, there are six kinds of affairs that people have which he humorously defines as: The "It's-Only-Lust" Affair (the most common type which is mostly about sex); The "I'll-Show-You" Affair (having an affair as a form of revenge against their partner); The "Just-In-The-Head" Affair (no sex involved); The "All-In-The-Family" Affair (having an affair with a partner's sibling); The "It's-Not-Really-An-Affair" Affair (where the participants believe they will eventually leave their partners so that they can be together); and the most dangerous type, The "Mind-Body" Affair (which feels emotionally, sexually, intellectually, and spiritually complete). In my opinion, different "types" of affairs lend themselves to varied feelings of guilt or remorse. The "Just in the Head" affair, for instance, which involves no sex, could result in no feelings of remorse because the participants might feel that, since there is no sex involved, it's no big deal. The "It's Only Lust" affair, on the other hand, includes that most taboo of topics—sex—which the 92% of Gallop poll respondents so vehemently abhor.

Something that must be taken into consideration when determining the potential impact an affair might have on one's spouse or partner is the spouse or partner's *knowledge* of the affair. The affair-having participants must determine whether or not to share the news of the affair with their spouse or partner, knowing that this knowledge will impact the spouse or partner to varying degrees. If, for instance, a person is in an "open marriage," wherein the couple agrees that it's okay to have extramarital relations, then the impact of the knowledge might be minimal. But if the affair-having person is married to a devout Mormon, the knowledge of the affair might be devastating. These are factors that a person should take into consideration as they make the decision whether to engage in an extramarital affair or not, for these considerations will help the person determine if it is in his or her self-interest.

It is not my place to determine whether having an affair is absolutely wrong or if it is acceptable; that is a decision that has to be made by the people considering the activity. I am saying, however, that if a person believes it to be in his or her self-interest (that's right, *her* self-interest: as many as 70% of women are believed to have had an extramarital affair), and if they have engaged in a decision support activity like completing a Pepper Tree chart (including the honest consideration of the *risks* and *impact on others*) and they still think it's right for them, then they should just say "What the f**k!" and go for it. I say this because any motivated behavior, including engaging in an affair, is a channel through which basic needs are simultaneously expressed or satisfied. And in the case of an affair, people are trying to satisfy some deficiency need such as the need for affection, love, or companionship. Having an affair signifies that there is some problem or issue within the relationship; something is missing or unfulfilling—such as sexual intimacy, for example. Human beings act to satisfy needs, so when these types of issues exist in a relationship (assuming the couple is unable to resolve them), then it can be understood why someone would look outside of the relationship to satisfy these deficiency needs. And when a person's (deficiency) needs are satisfied and the person receives pleasure from the activity that satisfied the needs, that person will be happier, his or her happiness will spread to others, those people will become more cooperative and more productive, and society will ultimately improve as a result.

In addition to feeling justified in some circumstances, having an affair can be psychologically healthy, too. According to research, an affair can provide positive feelings of belonging, affirmation, feeling attractive, restoring vitality, and improving one's outlook on life. These feelings can make a person feel valued and can also help a person renew an existing relationship with his or her current spouse or partner. So when having an affair is viewed from the vantage point of the person engaging in the affair, and when we take into consideration that the person may be satisfying some deficiency in his or her existing relationship, we can begin to acknowledge that all affairs are not created equal and some of them can be elegantly rationalized.

In The Pepper Tree Work Chart, this *Impact on others* category has a rating scale of '10' ("Positive" impact on others) to '0' ("Negative" impact on others). This is a category which the person completing The Pepper Tree Work Chart must consider *honestly*. If the person *wants* to believe that having an extramarital affair would have a *neutral* impact on his or her spouse or partner (whether the affair is revealed or not), but deep down inside, *knows* the affair would have a *negative* impact on the spouse or partner, then the person completing the chart should rate the impact *honestly* and give it a low score.

The overall attractiveness of engaging in the decision action (Go/No-Go)

After having considered and scored the expected value of your chosen course of action, the resulting amount of pleasure and happiness you expect to receive, and the expected impact of your decision, you should then add up all of the scores you gave to the various elements of the work chart to arrive at a total score (in the far right-hand column of the chart) between 0 and 80. Depending on the total score you arrived at, The Pepper Tree Work Chart will indicate that you should consider engaging in the activity (a score of 41 to 80), flip a coin (a neutral score of 40), or reconsider engaging in the activity (a score of 0 to 39). Based on the model, a neutral score of 40 implies that the activity you are considering won't negatively impact you or anyone else, but, at the same time, it might not provide you with any worthwhile or expected benefit either. I am not stating that if The Pepper Tree Work Chart which you complete for a decision action results in a score of 41 to 80 that you should engage in it (remember, there is an implicit assumption that you, the decision-maker, are *rational*) or that if it results in a score of 0 to 39 you should not engage in the decision action; those decisions are completely at your discretion. What I am saying, however, is that if you are rational and if you honestly complete a Pepper Tree Work Chart, the score that results will be a useful second opinion in determining if engaging in the activity is in your self-interest, and if doing so will likely provide you with the pleasurable experience and satisfaction you are hoping to achieve.

Decision-Making Using the Pepper Tree Work Sheet

Example: Bobby's Got the Munchies

I will take you through an example of how to use The Pepper Tree Work Chart to help you determine if engaging in an activity is in your self-interest. If it is, then, "What the f**k!" go for it. If not, then reconsider.

NOTE: Following this example will be more valuable if you do so while viewing a Pepper Tree Work Chart.

THE PEPPER TREE

THE PEPPER TREE WORK CHART

The Consideration _____ Score _____

Why Consider	Need Type	Value of the Choice	Impact on Higher Need	Experience	Pleasure Amount	Risk Level	Happiness Impact	Impact on Others	TOTAL SCORE
Need		High	Low	Lots	High	Low	Positive	Positive	Consider
10	**Basic** — Food, Shelter, Water, Sleep, Oxygen	10	10	10	10	10	10	10	80
9		9	9	9	9	9	9	9	72
8	**Safety** — Security, Stability, Order, Physical Safety	8	8	8	8	8	8	8	64
7		7	7	7	7	7	7	7	56
6	**Love** — Affection, Identification, Companionship	6	6	6	6	6	6	6	48
5		5	5	5	5	5	5	5	40
4	**Esteem** — Self-respect, Prestige, Success, Respect	4	4	4	4	4	4	4	32
3		3	3	3	3	3	3	3	24
2	**Actualize** — Self-fulfillment, Understanding, Achievement	2	2	2	2	2	2	2	16
1		1	1	1	1	1	1	1	8
Want		Low	High	None	Low	High	Negative	Negative	Reconsider
0		0	0	0	0	0	0	0	0

2012 Tab Edwards

201

CHOCOLATE PEPPERS

After a night of eating chocolate peppers while celebrating his fifth wedding anniversary with his wife, Bobby got the munchies. No, he wasn't starving; he just craved something on which to snack. So he gets out of bed, puts down the turkey baster, and heads to the kitchen to review his options. When he looks into the refrigerator and the cabinets, he notices that he has lots of options that will satisfy his munchies: vegetables, fruit, fish, poultry, meat, French fries, cookies, ice cream, Jell-O, candy, and donuts. "Ahh! *Donuts!*" he exclaims. So he decides to go for the donuts, but he feels kinda guilty about it.

Bobby is not an obese man and his health is good overall, but he has noticed that his pants have begun to fit a bit more snugly lately and he's worried that he is on the verge of gaining lots of "married weight." But damn! That donut was screaming his name. So between his wife's screams of "More milk, hurry!", the donut's screams of "Eat me … but get the chocolate peppers off your tongue first!", and Bobby's waistline saying "Don't do it … don't do it!", Bobby had a decision to make. So he whipped out a Pepper Tree Work Chart and applied his desire to eat the donut to the model to help him determine if eating it was a good thing to do. His rating of each element of the tool is provided below, along with his rationale for rating each element as he did.

Consideration: Whether or not to eat the donut

Element	Score	Rationale
Why consider taking an action? Need vs. Want	5	Bobby wants to eat the donut because he has the munchies, not because he is genuinely hungry. So his desire for the donut is more of a "want" (rated lower on the scale because it is a luxury rather than a primary physiological need) than it is a "need". However, since—as I have heard—the munchies are a manifestation of the hunger sensation, then having the munchies (the reason why he is considering eating the donut) is somewhere in the middle.
The type of need being addressed	N/A	Bobby is experiencing a form of hunger (the munchies), and his hunger indicates a physiological need for food. Bobby was presented with a wide selection of food items with which to satisfy his hunger; the foods range from vegetables to candy, any of which could satisfy his munchies. Bobby wants the donut (pastry).
The relative value of the options/ choices available to satisfy the need	4	Relative to some of the other food items available to Bobby (e.g. vegetables, fruit, and fish) the donut provides far less value (changes in welfare). Hunger satisfaction requires nutrition, and the nutritional value of a donut (sugar, dough, and oil) is less than that of vegetables ('10' points), but more than the nutritional value of candy (all sugar; '0' points).

Element	Score	Rationale
The impact of the options for satisfying a primary need on a higher-level need	7	Eating the donut could have an impact on one of Bobby's higher-level needs. Since Bobby is becoming concerned with gaining "married weight," he is starting to think about his esteem needs of self-respect and the respect of others. By eating the donut, Bobby will be contributing to his weight gain. And if Bobby gets "fat," he believes other people might look at him differently and in a less favorable light. (Hey, I don't make the rules, I'm just stating the facts: In America, fit people are perceived more favorably than those who are not). So while eating the donut could eventually have an impact on Bobby's esteem needs, for now, he's not that concerned about it.
The subject's experience with the chosen options	10	Bobby's favorite junk food is donuts, and he has been eating them since he was a boy. He keeps a supply of Krispy Kremes in his cupboard at all times.
The amount of pleasure expected to be received from the decision action	10	Being his favorite junk food, Bobby is well aware of the immense amount of pleasure he can expect to receive from eating the donut.
The risks associated with the options	8	Bobby is in overall good health and is not uncomfortably-overweight, so while there is some risk associated with eating the donut (e.g. weight gain, tooth decay, lethargy), it is relatively low (since this a reversed scale, a rating of '10' implies a low risk, while a rating of '0' implies a high risk).

Element	Score	Rationale
Happiness impact: the degree of happiness expected to be derived from the decision action	8	Bobby loves donuts, and when he eats them he experiences what can only be described as bliss—kinda like me when I eat vanilla creme sandwich cookies … yum! Eating donuts brings Bobby pleasure and a sense of immediate happiness. But because of the little voice in the back of his head saying "Don't do it … don't do it!," he does feel a small amount of guilt.
The impact of the decision on others	6	On the surface, it would not appear that eating a donut could in any way impact other people. For instance, Bobby is not diabetic, so there is no imminent risk that his wife or the hospital system would have to intervene should he eat the donut and get sick. But eating the donut doesn't have a positive impact on anyone else, either. So, for Bobby, eating the donut would have a neutral impact on other people. However, because it will make him happy, that happiness will positively impact others (which will ultimately be good for society and the world), so the rating is slightly better than a neutral rating of '5'.

Element	Score	Rationale
The overall attractiveness of engaging in the decision action (go/no-go)	58	When Bobby adds up all of the rating scores from the various elements of The Pepper Tree Work Chart, he will calculate a sum total score of 58. On the Total Score rating scale, any activity that scores above 41 should be considered by the decision-maker as a viable option in which to engage. And since the option of eating the donut to satisfy his munchies scored 58, Bobby should act in his self-interest and eat the donut because, in the end, eating that donut will make him happy and his happiness will spread to others. People will become more cooperative and productive, resulting in the betterment of society and the world.

THE PEPPER TREE

Bobby's completed work chart is provided below.

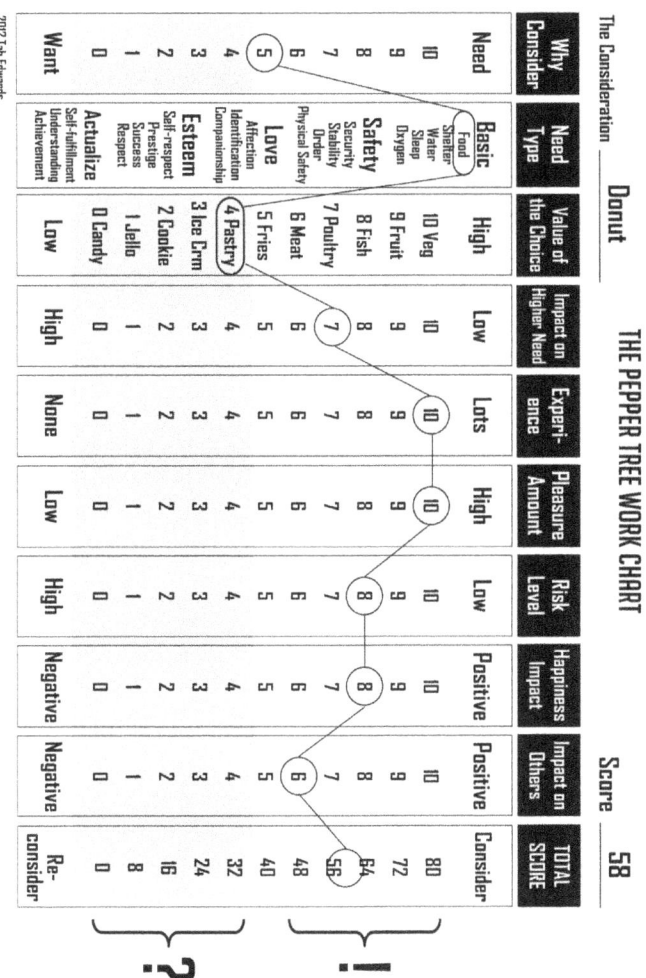

But what if Bobby was a badass and, one night at a celebrity-studded Las Vegas nightclub, he decided to test his machismo and instigate a fight with former heavyweight boxing champion Mike Tyson, who was in attendance? Would that be a rational thing to do? Bobby's Pepper Tree Work Chart would suggest not.

Consideration: Boosting self-esteem by instigating a fight with Mike Tyson

Element	Score	Rationale
Why consider taking an action? Need vs. Want	2	Bobby wants to take Mike Tyson on in a street fight in order to boost his self-esteem and impress upon his wife that he is a badass. Considering that Bobby is 5'3" tall and weighs about 160 pounds, it is reasonable to assume that he has a "Napoleon Complex" (named after the Emperor Napoleon of France, it commonly refers to men who are short in stature and is characterized by overly-aggressive and domineering behavior). So does Bobby "need" to fight or does he simply "want" to fight? Since Bobby is not defending his wife's honor and since Mike Tyson has done nothing to offend him, let's assume that Bobby just "wants" to fight.
The type of need being addressed	N/A	Bobby has a need to show that, although he is small in stature, he is no less of a man than anyone else, including the self-proclaimed "baddest man on the planet." This reflects a deficiency in an esteem need, such as a need for the respect of others, self-respect, and prestige.

Element	Score	Rationale
The relative value of the options/choices available to satisfy the need	0	As a patron in the Las Vegas nightclub, Bobby has several options available to him as outlets through which he can prove his manliness. He can drink shots of vodka without wincing, he can—with his wife's permission—test his pick-up skills on gorgeous women, he can arm-wrestle other customers, he can challenge someone to a foot race, he can bench-press his wife into the air, or ... he can fight Mike Tyson. Of all the options available to Bobby, fighting Mike Tyson holds little value for Bobby and would do even more damage to his self-respect, pride, reputation, and the respect he gets from others.
The impact of the options for satisfying a primary need on a higher-level need	3	Mike Tyson is 5'11" tall and weighs 250 pounds. Bobby is 8 inches shorter and 100 pounds lighter—and Bobby has never been the undisputed knock-out artist heavyweight boxing champion of the world. If this fight were to take place, there is a high probability that Bobby would be injured for life. If that happened, he could never be self-fulfilled, which means that fighting Mike Tyson would significantly impact Bobby's ability to achieve self-actualization.

CHOCOLATE PEPPERS

Element	Score	Rationale
The subject's experience with the chosen options	1	Although Bobby has been in several bar fights in his day, he has never squared-off against a professional boxer ... a professional heavyweight boxer ... who was the world's champion ... who outweighs him by 100 pounds ... and who is crazy! So while Bobby does have experience with fighting, he has absolutely no experience fighting anyone like Mike Tyson.
The amount of pleasure expected to be received from the decision action	0	*Pleasure?* Ha, ha, ha, ha, ha!
The risks associated with the options	0	Hmm ... let's see: humiliation, pain, broken bones, dentures, medical bills, bankruptcy, divorce, brain damage, coma, and death by suicide. These are all possible risks associated with Bobby's desire to fight Mike Tyson.
Happiness impact: the degree of happiness expected to be derived from the decision action	3	*Happiness?* Really? I will say, however, that, if he survives the fight and can remember his own name, he will have earned some bragging rights and can tell his family and friends that he actually fought Mike Tyson.

Element	Score	Rationale
The impact of the decision on others	3	If Bobby fought Mike Tyson, his wife—assuming she decides not to divorce him—would have to care for him the rest of his life. His medical bills could bankrupt him—compelling his extended family to pay his expenses—the hospital's physicians would have to commit time caring for him at the expense of other patients, and everyone would be miserable.
The overall attractiveness of engaging in the decision action (go/no-go)	12	The overall attractiveness of fighting Mike Tyson? Three words: Mitch "Blood" Green.

Needless to say, fighting Mike Tyson appears to be a bad idea for Bobby.

CHOCOLATE PEPPERS

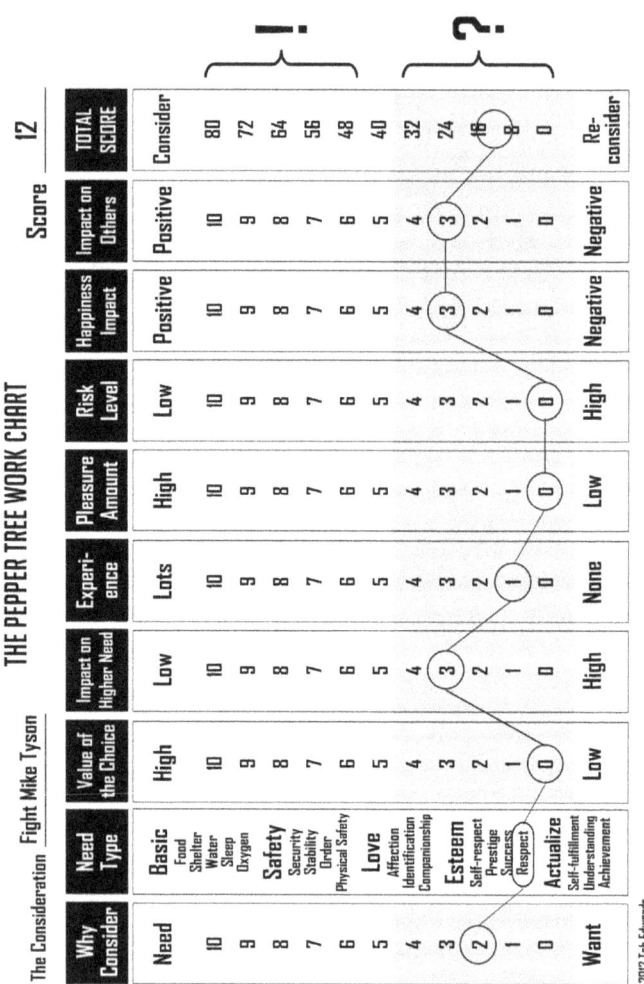

And The Pepper Tree for my purchase of the $5,000 suit? BAM!! A 60-point score! I feel vindicated for acting in my self-interest and purchasing that over-priced suit that I didn't really "need" but only "wanted".

Element	Score	Rationale
Why consider? Need vs. Want	2	I have many other suits, so I didn't "need" the suit, but I did really "want" it.
The type of need being addressed	N/A	I'll admit it: I wanted to look good and feel good to satisfy an esteem need (prestige, respect).
The relative value of the options/ choices	6	There are other things I could have spent the money on to gain a prestige-bump (such as renting a Ferrari for a day), but I coveted none of them as much as the suit.
The impact on a higher-level need	9	The suit purchase had little-to-no impact on a higher-level need.
The subject's experience with the chosen options	10	I have several great, high-quality suits, and lots of experience with them.
The amount of pleasure expected to be received	10	I used to fantasize about owning that suit. 'Nuff said.
The risks associated with the options	9	Not many, other than a significant reduction in my disposable income — which could come back to haunt me at some point.
Happiness impact	8	The only reason why I couldn't be happier about the purchase of the suit is because I have purchased other great suits in the past, so the thrill of the "great suit purchase" had diminished — just a little.

Element	Score	Rationale
The impact of the decision on others	6	The money involved ($5,000) didn't impact my family too much. However, because I felt great in the suit, it helped me perform better, which helped my audience improve their performance. I rated it a '6' because that is an indirect impact of the suit purchase; otherwise the impact would have been rather neutral.
The overall attractiveness of engaging in the decision action	60	When you complete a Pepper Tree Work Chart for a decision and you get a Total Score of 60—as I did with the suit purchase decision—what the f**k!, go for it. Because, in the end, that decision will be good for you, your loved ones, your community, society, and the world.

THE PEPPER TREE

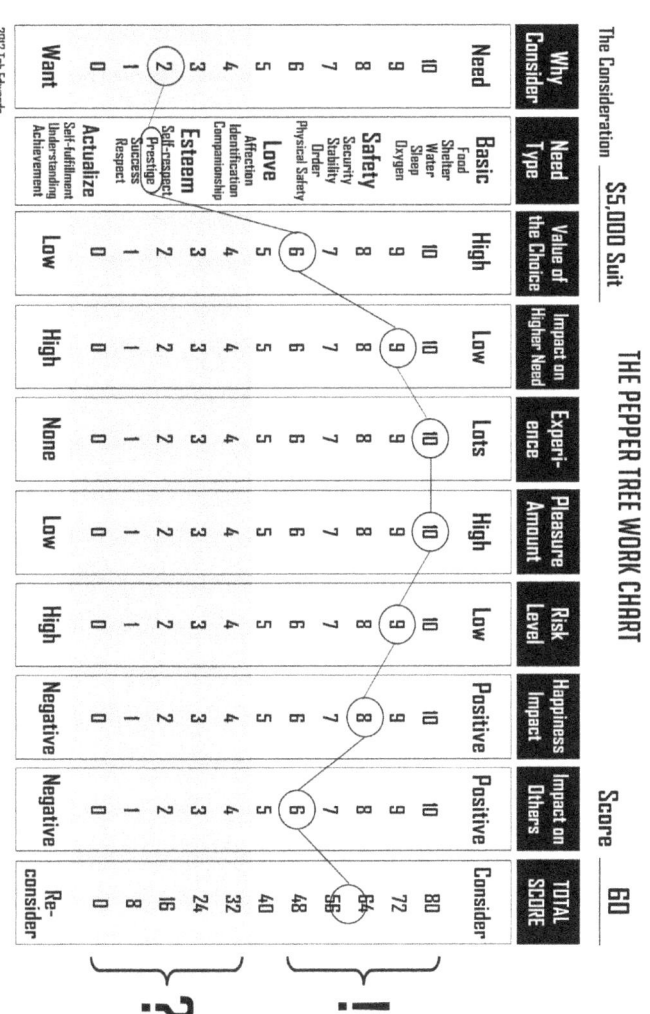

CHAPTER

5 TIPS FOR ENJOYING YOURSELF AND BEING BETTER

[The following chapter is excerpted from my original "Being Better" program series: *Being Better: A Strategy for Enjoying Yourself and Leading a More Fulfilling, Less Miserable Life*]

Imagine how cool it would be if more people actually spent their lives enjoying themselves and stopped being miserable killjoys. When people enjoy themselves, it implies that they are in possession of something or are engaging in an activity that provides them with a sense of pleasure and satisfaction. And, as I have stated throughout this book, pleasure contributes to one's general happiness, which spreads to other people, which bodes well for society and the world.

If *happiness* lies at one end of the "feelings" spectrum, then *misery* certainly lies at the other. Miserable people are considered to be dissatisfied and *unhappy*. And just as happy people tend to spread their happiness to others, the same applies to those who are miserable. People who are miserable often want other people to be miserable, too, and will drag them down into their realm of pessimism, resentment, hopelessness, and general unhappiness (ever heard the term "Misery loves company"?). The result is a negative impact on their fellow man, a negative impact on society, and, ultimately, a negative impact on the world.

The Feelings Scale

In order to begin the quest to lead a more enjoyable, fulfilling, and less miserable life, one must first understand how to avoid being miserable; this requires an understanding of why miserable people are miserable and how they became that way. If, for example, you wanted to know how to make a delicious cake, it would be helpful to know and avoid the pitfalls that cake-bakers experienced when their baking resulted in low quality, bad-tasting cakes. The same is true with enjoyment: If we want to know how to enjoy life and become more satisfied, it would be useful to identify the pitfalls of being miserable first so that we can avoid them.

Psychologist Jeffrey Bernstein, who has worked on this subject with individuals, couples, and families for more than twenty years, believes that there are two reasons why people become miserable: (1) Desperately wanting what you don't have; and (2) Desperately NOT wanting what you already have—with emphasis placed on the word DESPERATELY. Bernstein argues that aspiring to achieve goals in life beyond our current station is healthy, but aspiring to goals that are ridiculous and unachievable can lead to misery. For example, Billy is a 21-year-old college senior who plays on his school's junior varsity basketball team. He is 5'9" tall, cannot dunk the basketball, is a 60% free-throw shooter, and has not been able to crack the starting lineup on his *division III* school's team. Billy's lifelong goal—a goal he has aspired to since he was 8 years old—is to play professional basketball in the National Basketball Association (the NBA). Not the NBA's Development League (D-League), but the full-fledged NBA. Barring some miracle such as Billy waking up one morning and finding he has miraculously morphed into Dirk Nowitzki, it ain't happenin'. In this example, Billy does not have the talent or physical attributes to play professional basketball, and his irrational pursuit of an NBA career will lead to frustration, resentment of those who have achieved playing in the NBA, hopelessness, and general unhappiness, leading him to become miserable.

Overly not wanting what one *does* have is similar to overly wanting what you *don't* have, but there are also subtle differences. In the example of Billy the basketball player, although Billy does not have the talent to play basketball in the NBA, it's possible he does have the talent to play professional basketball at some level; there are lots of "professional" basketball leagues around the country, many of which—with his size and talent level—Billy could play in. But Billy doesn't *want* his current talent level, he wants LeBron James's, which means that, as long as he holds this lofty aspiration, he will remain miserable. Meanwhile, there are thousands of aspiring basketball players who would love to have Billy's talent and be able to play basketball at the division III collegiate level. If Billy could come to grips with the fact that he will never play basketball in the NBA but that he could still play professional basketball in other leagues, he could gain satisfaction and enjoyment from playing the game he loves.

The Role of Fear

Through my research I have found that there are many reasons why people are reluctant to act self-interestedly. The primary reasons are fear, guilt, remorse, and concerns for their reputation—with fear being the most predominant.

Fear (and being afraid) is an automatic response to stressful stimuli—we don't consciously trigger fear. It is a survival instinct intended to help humans survive dangerous situations by preparing us to either run for our life or fight for it; this is commonly referred to as the "fight or flight" response. In the course of human evolution, our ancestors, who were instinctive or lucky enough to fear the right things, survived to pass on their genes to subsequent generations. As their genes passed from generation to generation, the trait of "fear," and the "fight or flight" response to it, were selected as beneficial to the survival of the species.

If we didn't possess the ability to fear threatening stimuli or if we didn't have the capacity to be afraid, we as humans would not have survived for very long. When visiting the zoo we might jump into the lion's den to get a closer look and pet the cute, furry creatures. When seeing a train come speeding down the tracks at 100 miles per hour, we might be tempted to see if we can jump onto the front of it and go for a fast, exciting ride. We might walk to the top of The Empire State Building wearing a red cape and jump off just to see if the cape will make us fly like Superman. In humans, as in all animals, the purpose of fear is to promote survival.

As evolved human beings, we have learned which things to fear based on the expected unpleasantness that might be caused by the stimulus. And when we anticipate the awful things that might occur, we trigger a similar response to fear as if we were actually experiencing the fearful stimulus. It's like when kids know they are going to be spanked—their anticipation of the spanking will make them start crying before they actually get spanked, because they know what the spanking is going to feel like.

Generally speaking, people are uncomfortable with change and uncertainty. For the most part, we like and are more comfortable with the status quo. For this reason, we are reluctant to experience new things. Reluctance, like fear, is rooted deep in our physical nature and leads us away from change and new experiences, ideas, or possibilities, even if these things are ultimately good for us. Our reluctance to do, act on, or embrace new and different things keeps us in a state of stagnation, where progress, growth, and development are not possible. However, when we can overcome our natural reluctance and embrace all of the possibilities that this life holds, we can then move out of a stagnant state and move toward fulfillment and actualization.

When we are in the thick of the decision-making process, trying to decide whether or not to engage in a self-interested activity, we will anticipate the outcome of the engagement. Often, this anticipation can induce fear of one kind or another: Will I be subjected to physical harm or discomfort? Will I fail? Will I be rejected? Will I be punished? What will I lose? What will I have to sacrifice? Will I be abandoned and left alone? When we think this way, we often come to the conclusion that engaging in an activity will take us too far outside our comfort zone (change) or we simply become fearful of the potential outcomes we've been imagining. And as a result, we might decide not to engage in the self-interested activity.

It doesn't stop there. In addition to fear, we let guilt and remorse ("What will my actions take away from other people?" "Will this go against tradition or that which I have been taught?"); reputation ("What will the neighbors think?" "I'd be so embarrassed"); and other things ("How difficult will this be?" "Can I afford it?" "Am I capable of doing it?") hold us back from doing what we genuinely want and should be able to do.

Understandably, if you are physically unable (e.g. playing professional basketball in the National Basketball Association at 5'2" tall and with no prior basketball experience) or financially unable (e.g. owning a 2013 Bugatti Veyron 16.4 Grand Sport Vitesse automobile on a substitute teacher's salary) there are certain self-interested activities in which you may not be able to engage. However, for those activities that are tenable and within your grasp, overcoming the fear, guilt, and reputation concerns that you associate with engaging in the desired activities should become a priority. In most cases, this involves overcoming our fears and our reluctance to act.

Overcoming fear involves creating a conditioned response that counters the conditioned fear response. In other words, overcoming fear involves teaching ourselves to not be afraid of the cause of this fear. In the field of behavioral therapy, this is referred to as *exposure*—exposing oneself to the fear-inducing stimulus lessens one's anxiety when subsequently exposed to the stimulus. For example, if a person experiences Coulrophobia (the fear of clowns), it is likely because that person is experiencing what is known as the *uncanny valley effect*. The hypothesis of the "Valley" is that when the human features of a robot, doll, or a clown look and move almost like a real human being's, it creeps people out. So when people—especially children—see a clown, the clown looks like a normal person but the face is painted and it doesn't look quite right, so the child gets frightened.

To overcome Coulrophobia, a behavioral therapist might suggest that a parent let the frightened child occasionally paint the parent's face like a clown or remove clown makeup from a parent's painted face so that the child will teach and condition herself that the clown is nothing to be afraid of because it is just a person underneath the makeup and costume.

In the same way that people can condition themselves to overcome their fear of dogs, spiders, snakes, and numerous other animals, so too can people overcome their reluctance to experience new and different things. You want to take a much-needed vacation to an adult relaxation spa but you'd feel unbearably guilty about being away from the kids? A therapist might suggest that you start slowly: start by spending a half day away from them; then go away overnight; next, go away for a weekend; and then, take your week-long spa vacation. You can rest assured that the little ingrates will be just fine at home without you.

Each time we conquer our fear or overcome our reluctance to doing things that are in our self-interest, we get a little bit better at making our lives more enriched and fulfilling. And as we shift from hesitancy to acceptance, we open ourselves up to a world of possibility, a world of infinite potential to becoming fulfilled and experiencing all the great things that this world has to offer.

So, how does one go about acting in his or her own self-interest to achieve enjoyment, avoid becoming miserable, and, in the process, be happier and more fulfilled? There is no one single answer, approach, or set of practices that one can follow toward that end. That said, I have developed a simple ten-stage approach that can help people enjoy themselves, be more fulfilled and less miserable. My approach is based on research, observation, and—for what it's worth—my own opinions that have been shown to be effective and easy to implement.

Five abbreviated stages of my ten-stage *Being Better: A Strategy for Enjoying Yourself and Leading a More Fulfilling, Less Miserable Life* program are provided below. I personally selected these five stages of the program because they serve as the foundation for helping people get into the habit of acting in their self-interest, leading to greater happiness, fulfillment, and less misery.

Being Better: An Abbreviated Five-Stage Strategy

Stage One: Develop a "GODs" Model™

The GODs Model™—Goals, Objectives, Do Something—is not a religious concept, but is instead a model I defined to help people develop goals (business, professional, and personal) and the associated strategies to achieve those goals. Before proceeding, a few definitions are in order:

Goal: As defined in Chapter Five: *"Damn, I've Gotta Pee,"* a *goal* is the specific intended result of an activity or set of activities in which someone is engaged. It is a general statement of an intended outcome and it takes the form of an action statement: "To [action verb] [noun]". For example, a woman who is trying to lose weight might be doing so because she wants "to look good" for her 20-year high school reunion. In this example, the woman's goal might be defined as: *I want to look good for my high school reunion* (however she defines "good"). Another example might be a real estate agent whose goal is "to become the top real estate agent in Greater Los Angeles" (however "top" is defined).

As I wrote in Chapter Two: *The Joyful Relief of Happiness*, of the five elements that contribute to a person's well-being, *engagement* and *meaning* are the most crucial for leading a happy life. Goals give people a sense of purpose; they give life meaning. They provide people with hope, optimism about the future, confidence to pursue that which is possible, and the motivation to grow, develop, and better themselves and their station in life; goals give many people a reason to live.

And when a person successfully accomplishes a goal that he or she had defined for themselves, they not only realize the benefits that accompany the successful achievement of the goal (e.g. being the top real estate agent in Los Angeles), but they also gain the motivation to strive to be even better. In doing so, they move that much closer toward satisfying the need for self-actualization and becoming truly fulfilled in life.

Objective: An *objective* supports the goal. It answers the question: What specific thing(s) must I accomplish so that I will know that I have accomplished my goal? Objectives should be "S.M.A.R.T."— Specific, Measurable, Attainable, Realistic, and Time-bound—and there should be no wiggle room when it comes to determining whether or not a person has accomplished an objective. Following the example of the person who wants to become the top real estate agent in Greater Los Angeles, she might learn that in order to achieve this, her closed transaction volume for the year would have to exceed $161 Million. Armed with this knowledge, the real estate agent might define an objective as: "In order to become the top real estate agent in Los Angeles (the goal), I must sell $162 Million in closed transaction volume by December 31, 2014." Since the real estate agent knows the number she would have to attain, if she actually *does* exceed that target and sells the $162 Million that she defined as her objective (target), she will have accomplished her goal.

And the woman who is trying to lose weight because she "wants to look 'good' for her 20-year high school reunion" (her goal)? She might define her objective as: "I want to lose 15 pounds over the next 30 days" because she believes if she does so, she will look "good" and, therefore, will have accomplished her identified goal for the high school reunion—which is 30 days away. This implies, of course, that the only thing the woman needs to do in order to look "good" is to lose the weight. If true, then achieving her objective of losing 15 pounds would result in the accomplishment of her goal. If she finds, however, that losing the 15 pounds is not enough to make her look "good," then achieving her weight-loss objective would *not* result in the accomplishment of her goal. As a result, she would need to re-define what it will take to look "good," and possibly develop a second objective (such as: "To save $500 over the next 30 days, act in my self-interest, and purchase a fabulous dress—and shoes!—to complement my new look). This is consistent with the *Routing* element of my Rational Routing Routine whereby accomplishing activity "A" (in this example, "A" is the *objective*) will result in outcome "B" (accomplishment of the *goal*).

Do Something: After you have established a goal and the associated objectives that quantitatively and specifically define the goal, the next step is to *Do Something* to accomplish the objective(s) and, ultimately, the goal. This introduces the concept of **Strategy.** A strategy is a plan of action for how you will accomplish an objective and, consequently, the goal. It answers the question: What specific initiatives, activities, action items, and/or tasks must be completed in order to accomplish the associated objective? For the woman whose objective is lose 15 pounds in 30 days, she might determine that she must begin a weight-loss regimen (the initiative) that requires her to jog one mile each day (a task) and to consume less than 1,700 calories daily (a task). By following this weight-loss regimen, the woman will lose the 15 pounds within the 30-day window (accomplishing her objective), which will make her look "good" for the reunion (the goal).

So, if the woman follows a weight-loss regimen and successfully loses 15 pounds within the next 30 days, while also working over-time at her job so she can save $500 and purchase the dress and a pair of shoes, then the combination of the weight loss, the fabulous dress, and the new shoes will help to make her look "good" for the high school reunion. And, at that point, the woman will have successfully accomplished her goal. This accomplishment will make the woman feel better about herself and her achievement. As a result, she will gain more confidence—not only because of her improved physical self, but also because she knows that she can accomplish whatever she puts her mind to—and, most importantly, she will move a step closer to self-actualization and being the best that she can be.

Example: The GODs Model™ for the woman who wants to look "good" for her high-school reunion.

Goal	
To look "good" for my 20-year high school reunion	
Objective 1	**Objective 2**
To lose 15 pounds over the next 30 days	To save $500 over the next 30 days, act in my self-interest, and purchase a fabulous dress—and shoes!—to complement my new look

5 TIPS FOR ENJOYING YOURSELF & BEING BETTER

Do Something 1	Do Something 2
Begin a weight-loss regimen	Work one extra hour per day of overtime so that I can earn the extra money
Jog one mile each day	
Consume less than 1,700 calories daily	
By When 1	**By When 2**
Starting today; completed by 30 days	Beginning Monday; completed within 30 days
Beginning tomorrow; completed by 30 days	
Beginning tomorrow; completed by 30 days	

The relationships between the elements of the GODs Model™ are graphically represented in the diagram below:

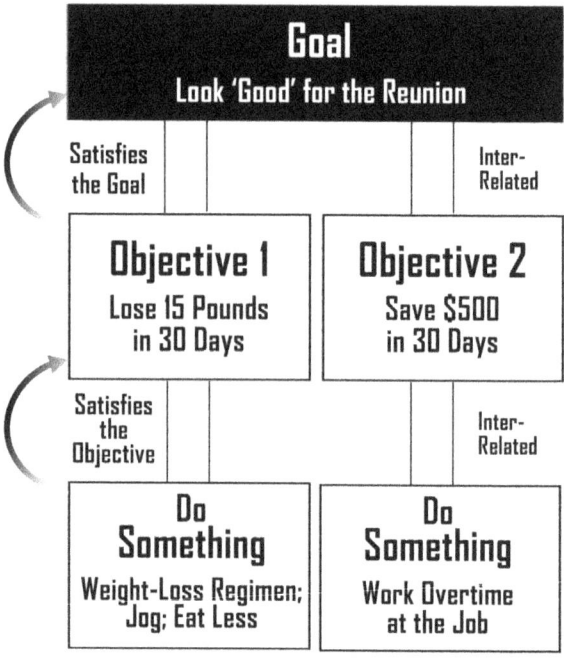

Stage Two: Avoid Falling Into Misery Traps

As I described at the beginning of this chapter, not only does being miserable suck, but, because "misery loves company," when we are miserable, we also bring others down with us into our pit of resentment, hopelessness, and general unhappiness. But if we become aware of what makes people miserable (and therefore unhappy), we have a better chance of avoiding the misery traps, thus improving our prospects for being more fulfilled. To help in this effort, I have provided some of the common misery traps and their associated misery-avoidance tips in the table below.

Misery Trap	Misery Avoidance Tip
Thinking negatively and being pessimistic	Focus on possibilities rather than limitations; it'll open up opportunities you might not otherwise discover.
Being jealous of other people and resentful of everything	Don't define yourself by others or base your progress in life on that of others. Define yourself for yourself. Appreciate what you are and what you have.
Wasting too much effort trying to change the things or people you cannot change	Focus on changing the things you can change; it'll reduce your feelings of hopelessness.
Focusing on problems and life's challenges	Focus on the post-problem state, define a way to get there, and relish life's possibilities.

Misery Trap	Misery Avoidance Tip
Considering your station in life (if you are unhappy with it and unfulfilled) to be permanent	Define a realistic vision of what you would like your station to be and develop a GODs Model™ to figure out how to get there.
Doing non-mandatory things for others at the expense of acting in your own self-interest	Follow the recommendations in this section of the Being Better: An Abbreviated Five-Stage Strategy chapter.
Hanging out with other miserable people	Get yourself some new friends.
Assuming that you are always right and that your way is the only way	Guess what? You're not and it's not! Continue to learn, associate with knowledgeable people, and seek truth. If you are honest with yourself and acknowledge that no one—not even you—is always right, you will open the door to admitting when you are wrong and begin valuing the contributions of others.
Holding grudges unnecessarily	Holding a temporary grudge is not necessarily a bad thing, depending on the circumstance. But eventually, you have to forgive or resolve or eat the loss, and eventually forget.
Simply living day-to-day with nothing that sparks a passion	Find a passion and dive in head-first. It will help give life meaning.

5 TIPS FOR ENJOYING YOURSELF & BEING BETTER

Stage Three: Force Yourself to be Happy, Whether You Like it or Not

We often get so caught up worrying about what other people think of us, putting the welfare of others before our own, believing that it's "better to give than to receive," and feeling responsible for the happiness of others at the risk of our own comfort, that we feel guilty about doing things for ourselves. Eventually, with many people, the normative behavior becomes sacrificing their own enjoyment in order to make other people happy and persuade their neighbors to think highly of them. Stop it! Life's too short to be miserable and not live it to the fullest. People have to take responsibility for their own happiness: You wanna go to the movies to see the midnight showing of "Nosferatu" but your husband doesn't want to go? Screw him; go by yourself. You want to take a vacation to Disney World to check out the new Fantasy Land expansion but your kids hate Disney World? Then leave their spoiled asses at home and go to Disney World by your *damn* self! You want to attend the annual Flower Show but your boyfriend is allergic to flowers and, therefore, doesn't want to go? Then call your back-up, second-string date, leave your Allegra®-sniffing loser of a boyfriend at home and go smell the roses. Husband done before you climax? Don't rely on him, take responsibility into your own hands—literally. Your girlfriend is mad at you and doesn't want to go out for drinks? Then follow the words of wisdom of that legendary Poet Laureate— Big Bank Hank of The Sugar Hill Gang: "If your girl starts acting up, then you take her friend." And you want to wear your Sly Stone silver platform Disco boots but you're afraid that your neighbors will ridicule you? Put on the boots, walk outside, go over to your neighbor's house, knock on their door, and when they answer, tell them to *kiss your ass*! You have to do things for *yourself*!

I know it's hard to behave this way when you have a family or other loved ones, but you must force yourself to be happy and not feel guilty about doing things because of what others will think or what you might be "taking away" from other people by following your own course. Your enjoyment and fulfillment is not a zero-sum game where the only way you can do things that *you* want to do is if someone else gets slighted; you must change that mindset. I have provided some recommendations below of things that you can do to help you change that mindset and get on the path to forcing yourself to be happy.

- **Live by *The Rule of 41*.** *The Rule of 41* is a rule that I defined which states: When trying to decide whether to act in your own self-interest and do something that provides you with pleasure, satisfaction, enjoyment, and/or happiness, complete a Pepper Tree Work Chart. For every activity that receives a score of 41 or higher, say "What the f**k!" and go for it. Because in the end, that decision will turn out to be good for you, your loved ones, society, and the world.

  Don't have time to create a Pepper Tree Work Chart? Then here's a short-cut: When deciding whether or not to engage in an activity, imagine you are the ruler of an island and you can do absolutely *anything* that you want to do without reproach. The only factors involved in the decision-making process are you and your sense of reason. Then ask yourself: Should I engage in this activity that I am considering? If you are rational and honest with yourself, you stand a good chance of making a useful decision. While this approach is in no way comparable to either the Rational Routing Routine for decision-making or the Pepper Tree process, it will provide better results than simply shooting first and asking questions later.

- **Create a "Guilty-Pleasure List"** (also known as a *Self-Interest List* and a *What the F**k! List*). By calling it a "guilty pleasure" list, you are acknowledging that it is a list of things that you would normally feel guilty about engaging in, even though they will (hopefully) bring you pleasure. And the more you look at your Guilty Pleasure list, the less power and impact the word "guilty" will have on your psyche and, eventually, you will begin to disassociate the activities on your list with this nagging, annoying feeling. I liken it to the word "geek." Prior to the Dot-com boom of the late 1990s, being called a "geek" was quite an insult. It implied that the person was an un-cool, nerdy, dorky, dufus bookworm who carried ink pens in a shirt pocket protector. But with the expansion of the Internet, the "geeks" started developing Internet-based services & companies, netting themselves millions of venture-capital and Initial Public Offering (IPO) dollars in the process, and catapulting them to rock-star status (does anyone *really* think that Facebook's Mark

Zuckerberg is cool? No!). Suddenly, it became cool to be a geek, and now nerdy, smart people everywhere are proud to wear that label.

By creating a Guilty-Pleasure List, you seize the opportunity to stop living vicariously through other people and start being the person you want to be by doing the things you've always dreamt about doing. Creating the list is not only fun, but it's also easy to do. First, brainstorm and write down a list of *everything* that you've ever wanted to do. One way to help generate ideas for your list is to consider this hypothetical question: If you knew that you were going to die tomorrow, what things would you look back on and regret not having done, experienced, or accomplished? Add those items to your Guilty-Pleasure List. As you brainstorm your list, don't worry about how much money engaging in the activity will cost, what your neighbors or family will think, the possible trade-offs associated with you engaging in the activity, or how selfish or how guilty you will feel; just create a laundry list of things that you want, have ever wanted, or might want (to do) in the future. Once you start your list, you will probably realize how much you are and have been missing out on in life by not acting in your self-interest and doing some of the things on your list.

Next, rank the items on your list based on how badly you want to do them—disregarding how much it will cost, what people will think of you, how neglected your family will be, or how guilty you will feel. So, if your Guilty-Pleasure List consists of 50 activities, the activity that you want to do more than any of the others would

5 TIPS FOR ENJOYING YOURSELF & BEING BETTER

be rated #1, and the activity you would want to do last would be rated #50. Once you have ranked your list of activities, create a Pepper Tree Work Chart for each, starting with your top ten. Remove any activities from your list that receive a Pepper Tree score of less than 41 total points. Then, re-rank the remaining activities based on their Pepper Tree point total scores, applying *The Rule of 41*. The logic behind using the chart is that the activities with the highest Pepper Tree scores should bring you the most satisfaction and happiness. Your Top 5 might look something like this:

Example: Bill's Guilty-Pleasure List

Activity	Original Ranking	Pepper Tree Score	Re-Ranking
Stroll through Time's Square in New York City on a Saturday afternoon in December, wearing pink hot-pants, roller blades, a mink stole, and a chef's hat, while singing "The Star Spangled Banner"	1	56	3
Take the General Educational Development (GED) exam just to see if I can pass it without even studying for it	2	44	4
Get married in the Church of the Flying Spaghetti Monster and see if anyone considers it to be legitimate and binding	3	63	2

Activity	Original Ranking	Pepper Tree Score	Re-Ranking
Call the 26-seat, super-exclusive New York city restaurant, Masa (with its $300-$500 prix-fixe menu), make a reservation using the name "T. Boone Pickens," and (1) see how pissed off they will be when I show up instead, and (2) if they even let me in	4	41	5
Verb the Noun while driving a car through midtown Manhattan in rush-hour traffic while listening to Barry Manilow and sipping a Slurpee ... again	5	67	1

Once your Guilty-Pleasure List has been edited and re-ranked, make it a priority to do at least one thing from your list each and every month without fail. In fact, I recommend creating a monthly *Do Diddly Day*: A total blow-off day where nothing is planned or structured. It is a day for *you*; a day to do whatever you want to do on your own terms and without any external influences, family responsibilities, or household chores to compromise your day of self-interest. Your wife wants to go to the movies on your Do Diddly Day? Tell her to go by herself. Your kids need a ride to the soccer game? Tell 'em to walk.

Having a day to yourself, a day to act completely in your own self-interest—unencumbered by any type of responsibility whatsoever—is healthy and often mentally needed. Taking a monthly Do Diddly Day will make you happier throughout the year, enabling you to spread happiness to other people at least once per month. Psychological research has shown that happiness is more strongly correlated with the *frequency* of satisfying events rather than with the intensity of the satisfying events. So, if you are happy more times than you are not, then, overall, you will live a happier life which will benefit you and others, too.

Stage Four: Do Not Let Others Define You or Your Actions

The self-proclaimed "black-lesbian feminist mother lover poet" Audre Lorde once stated: "If I didn't define myself for myself, I would be crunched into other people's fantasies for me and eaten alive." A great sentiment if ever there was one. What Lorde suggests by this statement is that people should feel free to be who they intrinsically want and choose to be, and they should not let other people determine that role for them. The consequences of allowing other people to define you include the potential for them to use you in whichever manner they choose. To them, you are what *they* want you to be and, since they have placed you in a particular role, they have the right to do with you what they will.

Another expression of being defined by other people is when you derive your happiness from the happiness that you provide to others, even if it means your own happiness comes second. Such people who are anxious to please other people by fulfilling their needs and expectations are called "People-Pleasers." People-pleasers thrive on the praise, adulation, and positive response they receive from the people they spend so much effort to please.

According to Linda Tillman, a psychologist at Emory University, people-pleasers are unable to gauge the value of their own actions, and "As a result, they spend their lives looking for validation from others." I think it is sad when a person believes that "If I don't please this person or these people, they will not like me." This behavior eventually becomes self-reinforcing, making the behavior difficult to change. The pattern of feeling valuable by complying with the demands of others can lead a person to lose sight of their own personal aspirations, leaving the people-pleaser to live an unfulfilled and even miserable life.

To be happy and fulfilled, we cannot be bullied by other people or controlled by external influences, especially when it is in our self-interest to do otherwise. In making decisions regarding *your* life and *your* happiness, consider only what your heart and mind covet, because you only get one shot at this life so you can't let anyone dictate the course of *your* life except you. Other than when you were a child, have you ever trusted anyone enough to allow them to make life-choices on your behalf and felt they could make these choices better than you could? Probably not. You and only you know what's truly in your heart and what you desire most in this world.

Do not conform to a way of thinking or behaving that other people define for you because you're concerned what they'll think of you if you do not conform. No one should create an identity for you or dictate your world view; that's your responsibility. Rational people should neither allow this nor allow anyone to chart the course of their life. If you do, then you are in a cult. Get out!! Your family is Christian but you want to practice Judaism? Then go get yourself a Torah. Your family is Jewish and you want to come out as an Atheist? Then put away your kippah; the late Christopher Hitchens would be proud. You want to come out to your parents as being gay but you fear their reaction? Then gather them in the kitchen and just blurt it out: "Mom, Dad … I called you here because I have something important to share with you. I'm gay." Your father is a leader in the Ku Klux Klan but you want to marry a Black man? Uh … good luck with that one. But just say "What the f**k!" and go out and get your man, and let the chips fall where they may. Remember: It's *your* life, and you must define yourself for yourself … or be eaten alive.

Stage Five: Don't Define Yourself Compared to Others

The idiom "Keeping up with the Joneses" refers to the way people use their neighbors' material acquisitions and social status as the benchmark by which they measure themselves and their social standing. Not keeping up with the Joneses means—to some people—that they are existing below some acceptable standard of wealth, status, and even equality. Screw the Joneses! By measuring yourself against the accomplishments, wealth, and status of other people, you are allowing them to indirectly define you. I believe that when you measure your station against that of other people, you are acknowledging that you are disappointed with your own station in life. Why does the fact that your neighbor drives a Mercedes Benz and you drive a Yugo make you feel inferior? Because it reminds you of just how cheap and inferior your car is and how relatively poor you are. It shouldn't, but it does. Why does it bother you that your neighbor hires a professional landscaping company to groom his lawn and you have to cut your own grass using a 14-inch, manual, $79 Economy Reel Mower? Because it reminds you of how much your own mower sucks … and how much less you have. It shouldn't, but it does. And why on earth does the fact that your neighbor vacations in the Hamptons and you can only afford to go to Wildwood, New Jersey for the day irk you? Because it makes you feel as though you have underachieved in life. It shouldn't, but it does. But look at the bright side: If your neighbor *does* vacation in the Hamptons, he's more than likely a pretentious mama's boy so there's a good chance you can kick his ass in a street fight! And THAT should remind you just how much more "manly" you are than he!

It's okay to admire someone's achievements and even aspire to reach those heights yourself. That's different than *measuring yourself* against other people and believing that, in order for you to no longer feel like a loser,

5 TIPS FOR ENJOYING YOURSELF & BEING BETTER

you have to match their accomplishments, wealth, and status. That type of envy and *overly wanting what you don't have* can lead to jealousy and resentment, two emotions that contribute to being miserable; and obviously, when you are miserable, you are not happy.

And don't *resent* anyone else's success, looks, wealth, or achievements either. Doing so won't improve *your* situation, it'll only make you miserable. Being jealous or envious is an expression of the disappointment you feel regarding your *own* progress, so, if anything, you should be angry at *yourself* instead of jealous of another person. Once you recognize that your jealousy doesn't help YOU, you can then begin to focus on fixing your perceived shortcomings. So acknowledge other peoples' success, give them credit for their accomplishments, aspire to do the best that *you* can do, and strive to achieve as much as *you* are capable of achieving; this will allow you to self-actualize. And once you do, it will become easier to accept that you are the best person you can be and that your life is not defined by other people.

CHAPTER

THE CHAIN OF SELF-INTEREST LINKED: A SUMMARY

10

Throughout this book, I have attempted to establish the causal linkage between a person acting in his or her self-interest in response to a human need and the positive impact resonated by those self-interested actions. My research revealed a causal relationship ("if A then B"), as opposed to a coincidental one, between a person's self-interested actions and the resultant positive impact for those people surrounding him or her, and, ultimately, the betterment of society. And this impact all begins with people acting to satisfy some basic human need.

Need

As I have stated throughout this book, all human behavior is aimed toward the satisfaction of some human need. Whether the need is a basic physiological one such as hunger, or a higher-level one such as the desire to fulfill our destiny and become all that we can be (a self-actualization need), we do things because we are attempting to satisfy a need and alleviate the discomfort we experience when that need is unmet.

Options

As we seek the satisfaction of a need, if we are fortunate, there are often an unlimited number of options available to us. If someone is hungry, there are thousands of food items that can satisfy that need. If the person is lonely, there are any number of ways to find companionship, ranging from Internet dating websites to pets. If the person wants to feel valued, there are thousands of options available to the person to help him or her improve their self-esteem, including on-line education options, fitness programs, charity work, and … $5,000 suits.

Decision

When we decide to act toward the satisfaction of a need and are presented with multiple options for doing so, we must make a decision among these available options. We do this by choosing the option that has the highest probability of not only satisfying the need, but bringing us pleasure as well. And as we begin to decide among the options available to us for satisfying a need, we must do so rationally and logically. Our decision-making process can be conscious or subconscious, meaning that it could be a routine that we follow without giving much thought to the mechanics—like breathing, for instance.

Because it is easier to spend the time needed to make a good decision up front than it is to resolve the consequences of a bad decision down the road, it only makes sense for us to conduct this process thoroughly. By following a decision-making routine, enlisting a decision-support tool like The Pepper Tree Work Chart, using our experience, or taking advantage of reference experience—the experience of other people who were confronted with the same issue we are—we can be sure to make decisions that satisfy our needs most efficiently, bring us pleasure, avoid pain or discomfort, and have the highest probability of being in our self-interest.

Self-Interest Action

After we have followed our normal, logical decision-making process and have decided on the "best" course of action toward the satisfaction of the need, we must then act on the decision by engaging in the activity that—however we arrived at it—we believe to be in our best (self) interest. This is most often determined by the decision option that will satisfy our need most efficiently and effectively and will make us feel good, while not "significantly" negatively impacting others in the process.

After we get over our unsubstantiated initial feelings of guilt at actually doing something for *ourselves*, we will pull the trigger and engage in the activity that has the highest likelihood of satisfying the need and bringing us material prosperity, emotional well-being, and/or personal fulfillment, all things that prompt one's happiness.

Need Satisfaction and Pleasure

If we have acted rationally in our decision-making (including following *The Rule of 41*) and have engaged in the activity that we determined to be in our self-interest, our actions should satisfy our initial need and bring us a feeling of pleasure, well-being, and simply make us feel good. All of these emotions should lead us to experience happiness.

Happiness

Generally, happiness is what we feel when our basic needs are met and we no longer find ourselves in a constant state of longing for that which we don't have.

The Spread of Happiness

As I wrote in Chapter Two: *The Joyful Relief of Happiness*, studies show that emotions can pass from person-to-person up to three degrees of separation away. The findings suggest that a person's happiness may be determined by how happy the person's friends' friends' friends are, even if some of these "friends" are total strangers to the person. In terms of happiness, everyday interactions we have with other people can be contagious. So, if a person acts in his or her self-interest and that activity makes the person happy, then that person's happiness will spread to others, providing them with a sense of happiness, too.

Cooperation & Productivity

Cooperation is often born of mutual self-interest on the part of multiple parties interacting with each other. When people cooperate, we develop new products and new solutions, and we even discover cures more quickly. As a result, societies benefit overall. When people cooperate, we are more productive, we perform better, and we contribute to the improved performance of businesses and institutions, enabling companies to employ more people, offer better products and services, and increase wealth—all things that have a positive impact on communities.

The Common Good

When we are happy, we have a tendency to engage in more prosocial behavior. Such acts of generosity and cooperation provide tangible benefits to people and communities, thereby contributing to the betterment of society.

As I described in Chapter Four: *The Goodness of Self-Interest*, Adam Smith wrote: "It is not from the benevolence of the butcher, the brewer, or the baker, that we expect our dinner, but from their regard to their own self-interest." Although the butcher established his butcher shop based on a self-interested decision to make profits—affording him the opportunity to live comfortably and more happily—his decision to do so benefits his community and therefore society by serving as a source of food for the shop's patrons and a source of additional tax revenue to the community. Ultimately, the butcher's self-interested decision to open the shop will contribute to the common good of his neighbors, his community, and society.

A Better World

It stands to reason that if people, groups, communities, neighborhoods, towns, cities, states, and societies in general are all better off, then this world will ultimately be a "better" one—"better" being defined as an improvement over some previous state or benchmark.

While acting in your self-interest could provide ancillary benefits to society, **the reason to act self-interestedly is for the direct benefits *you* will receive from doing so**. Self-interest—as the name implies—is about acting in a manner that is in *your* best interest and provides you with the benefits you expect to receive; benefits that will contribute to your general well-being and fulfillment as a person.

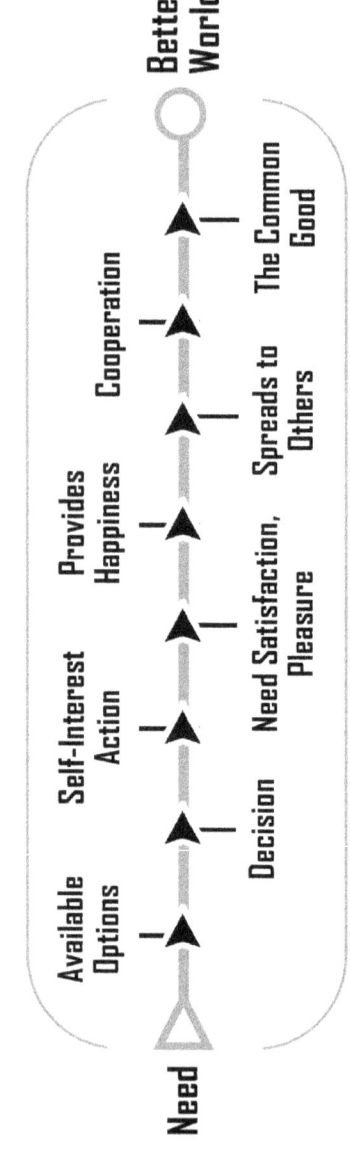

CONCLUSION

"Don't you ever get the feeling that all your life is going by and you're not taking advantage of it? Do you realize you've lived nearly half the time you have to live already?"

— Ernest Hemingway, *The Sun Also Rises*

This book started out as an exploration of the rationale behind the seemingly counterintuitive in-flight safety instruction advising adult passengers to secure their oxygen mask *first* before assisting their children with the children's masks. Although I have flown on airplanes hundreds of times over the years, I remember sitting on a flight to Paris, France when I first gave any thought to—okay, paid any *attention* to—what the flight attendants were instructing.

I'm not sure exactly why, but for some reason I thought about that standard, perfunctory instruction and its seemingly unnatural directive ("If you are traveling with a child or someone who requires assistance, secure your mask first, and then assist the other person") every time I would board an airplane, see an image of an airplane, or see any depiction of an airline flight. It got so bad that whenever I would watch the classic 1980 comedy movie *Airplane*, I wouldn't focus on my favorite part of the movie (an absolutely hilarious scene in which then-65-year-old white actress, Barbara Billingsley, says to the flight attendant who was having a hard time understanding the slang being spoken between two African-American male passengers: "Oh, stewardess, I speak jive. Jus' hang loose, blood. She gonna catch ya up on da' rebound on da' med side") but would, instead, think about that persistent in-flight instruction. And the more I thought about it, the more I wondered about other situations in which taking care of *yourself* first was not only good for you, but, because you were secure, your security contributed to the security and well-being of others around you also. Was this idea of ensuring your own well-being *first* only applicable to airline flights, or was it good for other activities in everyday life as well?

As I started researching the idea, I was encouraged (and a little surprised) to uncover lots of evidence and other data that support the idea that acting in one's own self-interest (e.g. first securing your own oxygen mask) can lead to an individual's happiness, and that happiness will spread to other people, making people and societies more cooperative and productive, eventually contributing to the betterment of society. This was not only interesting but refreshing, too. I have always been of the opinion that people expend too much time and effort focusing on the well-being, comfort, and happiness of others, often

CONCLUSION

at the expense of their own happiness and well-being. We should take greater responsibility for ensuring our own happiness and not give a damn what other people think of us for doing so; we should act more in our self-interest.

Some will call such an attitude "selfish," but, as I explored through this book, there is a difference between acting *selfishly* and acting in one's *self-interest*. Selfish says, "I'm going to use my entire paycheck to buy a new pair of shoes to wear to the club tonight" when your 2-year-old needs diapers and a baby sitter; self-interest says, "I'm going to use my paycheck to buy a pair of shoes to wear to the club tonight. And if I am going to the club, I will need to hold some money back to pay for a babysitter and diapers."

If this decision of whether or not to spend the entire paycheck on a pair of shoes was considered with the assistance of a Pepper Tree Work Chart, the club-goer would arrive at one of two outcomes: (1) Get a sub-40 point score on The Pepper Tree Work Chart, indicating that spending the entire paycheck on a pair of shoes and leaving your diaper-less 2-year-old home alone is a bad idea; or (2) get a score of 41 points or higher, indicating that using the paycheck to buy the shoes is good, because the decision-maker also considered the babysitter and the diapers. That's the value of The Pepper Tree and The Pepper Tree Work Chart: Using the tool can help people make decisions that are in their self-interest and reconsider decisions that are possibly selfish. Yes, it's a simple tool and it's not perfect, but it does help and it's cheaper than a psychiatrist.

All human behavior is directed toward the satisfaction of some need. When we eat, we are trying to satisfy the physiological need of hunger, and when we educate ourselves, we are trying to satisfy an esteem need (prestige, success, and/or the respect of others) or self-actualization (understanding and/or achieving one's own potential). When we act of our own free will, making intrinsic decisions unencumbered by some external influence, we will usually act in our self-interest. And when we do, we will become more fulfilled.

When you consider that Earth is approximately 4.5 billion years old, you can get an appreciation for just how transitory a human life is. The oldest living human is just a pimple on the earth's 4.5 billion-year-old ass. So, for you and me, we are relative gametes; our time on earth is fleeting in the relative scheme of things.

Our lives are far too short not to get the most out of them, and we cannot get the most out of life if we succumb to the external influences that preclude us from doing those things that we want to do; things that will bring us pleasure, make us happier, and help us to become more fulfilled during our brief time on this planet. It's time to change the conversation from "I wish I woulda" to "I'm glad I did." So go ahead. Follow the *Abbreviated Five-Stage Strategy* for being better. Shed that cloak of guilt. Flip your reluctance the middle finger. Scan your Guilty-Pleasure List, say "What the f**k!" and start ticking off your Top 5. Your neighbors might frown upon you, and your family might not like that you are no longer spending every waking hour focused on and catering to

CONCLUSION

them. Screw them all! This is *your* life and you have an obligation to dictate the terms of it. It's time to start making decisions for YOU and not feel guilty about it. When you do, you will start to live a more pleasure-filled existence, you will be happier, your life will be more purposeful and fulfilled, and your family, loved ones, friends, and community will all be better off as a result.

ABOUT THE AUTHOR

Tab Edwards is the author of seven books and is considered one of the most creative, engaging, and entertaining speakers in the country. He has worked with thousands of people and businesses around the world to become more effective at accomplishing their goals and "better" at whatever their pursuit.

His workshops, coaching sessions, seminars, and speaking engagements are highly regarded and have been delivered to general audiences and professionals at companies around the world, including IBM Corporation, AT&T, Pfizer, Hewlett-Packard, Drexel University, Halliburton, Staples, Amtrak, and Citigroup to name a few.

SELECTED BIBLIOGRAPHY

INTRODUCTION

Altman LK. *Who goes first? The story of self-experimentation in medicine*. New York: Random House; 1987.

Ameisen, Olivier. *The End of My Addiction*. New York: Sarah Crichton Books, Farrar, Straus and Giroux, 2009.

Grant, B., D. Dawson, F. Stinson, S. Chou, M. Dufour, and R. Pickering. "The 12-month Prevalence and Trends in DSM-IV Alcohol Abuse and Dependence: United States, 1991–1992 and 2001–2002." *Drug and Alcohol Dependence* 74.3 (2004): 223-34.

Schofield, Hugh. "France Abuzz over Alcoholic 'cure'" BBC News. BBC, 12 June 2008. 05 May 2013. http://en.wikipedia.org/wiki/Olivier_Ameisen.

"Twelve-month Prevalence of DSM-IV Alcohol Abuse by Age, Sex, and Race-ethnicity: 2001–2002." *Twelve-month Prevalence of DSM-IV Alcohol Abuse by Age, Sex, and Race-ethnicity: 2001–2002*. 05 May 2013.

Chapter One:
THE $5,000 SUIT

Bakalar, Nicholas. "Many Don't Wash Hands After Using the Bathroom." *The New York Times*. The New York Times, 27 Sept. 2005.

Biddle, Jeff E., Hamermesh, Daniel S. "Beauty and the Labor

Market." *The American Economic Review*, Volume 84, Issue 5 (1994), 1174-1194.

Campbell-Meiklejohn, Daniel, Dominik Bach, Andreas Roepstorff, Raymond Dolan, and Chris Frith. "How the Opinion of Others Affects Our Valuation of Objects." *Frontiers in Behavioral Neuroscience* (2010): Vol. 20, Issue 13, pp. 1165-1170.

Dion, Karen, Ellen Berscheid, and Elaine Walster. "What Is Beautiful Is Good." *Journal of Personality and Social Psychology* 24.3 (1972): 285-90.

"Do Attractive People Get Better Treatment Than Others?" *Jet*, Sept 3, 2001.

Dobson, Roger. 13 August 2007. "Beautiful people earn 12% more than Ugly Bettys". *The Independent.* http://www.independent.co.uk/news/science/beautiful-people-earn-12-more-than-ugly-bettys-461261.html

Fowler, J. H., and N. A. Christakis. "Dynamic Spread of Happiness in a Large Social Network: Longitudinal Analysis over 20 Years in the Framingham Heart Study." *Bmj* 337.Dec04 2 (2008): A2338.

Hershberger, Paul J. "Prescribing Happiness: Positive Psychology and Family Medicine." *Family Medicine* (2005): 630.

Louis, Catherine Saint. "The Great Unwashed." *The New York Times*. The New York Times, 31 Oct. 2010.

Lyubomirsky, Sonja, Laura King, and Ed Diener. "The Benefits of Frequent Positive Affect: Does Happiness Lead to Success?" *Psychological Bulletin* 131.6 (2005): 803-55.

Patricelli, Kathryn. "Why Do Adults Stay In Abusive Relationships?" *Mental Health Care, Inc.* http://www.mhcinc.org/poc/view_doc.php?type=doc&id=8483

Seligman, Martin E. P., and Jane Gillham. *The Science of Optimism and Hope: Research Essays in Honor of Martin E.P. Seligman*. Philadelphia: Templeton Foundation, 2000.

Snyder, C. R., and Shane J. Lopez. *Handbook of Positive Psychology*. Oxford: Oxford UP, 2005.

BIBLIOGRAPHY

Chapter Two:
THE JOYFUL RELIEF OF HAPPINESS

"Happiness Improves Health and Lengthens Life." *U.S. News.* March 3, 2011. http://www.usnews.com/science/articles/2011/03/03/happiness-improves-health-and-lengthens-life

McCarthy, Ryan. "Daniel Kahneman, Nobel Prize Winner: Happiness Can Be Bought For About $60,000 Per Year." *Huffington Post*, May 25, 2011. http://www.huffingtonpost.com/2010/06/04/daniel-kahneman-nobel-pri_n_601236.html

"Meaning of happiness." *This Emotional Life. PBS.com.* http://www.pbs.org/thisemotionallife/topic/happiness/what-happiness

Park, Alice. "The Happiness Effect." *Time*. Dec. 11, 2008. http://www.time.com/time/magazine/article/0,9171,1865960,00.html#ixzz2SBNj5yh7

Seligman, Martin. *Flourish: A Visionary New Understanding of Happiness and Well-Being.* New York: Atria Books, 2012.

Chapter Three:
"WHY DID I BUY THAT SUIT?"

Deci, Edward L., and Richard M. Ryan. *Intrinsic Motivation and Self-determination in Human Behavior.* New York: Plenum, 1985.

Deci, Edward L., and Richard M. Ryan. "The "What" and "Why" of Goal Pursuits: Human Needs and the Self-Determination of Behavior." *Psychological Inquiry* 11.4 (2000): 227-68.

Deci, Edward L.; Flaste, Richard; *Why We Do What We Do: Understanding Self-Motivation.* Penguin Books; Reprint edition (1996).

Itkin, Igor. "Top 10 Rebels Throughout History." *Listverse.com.* May 17, 2011.

BIBLIOGRAPHY

Johnson, Jone L. "Audre Lorde Quotes." *About.com*, Women's History. http://womenshistory.about.com/od/quotes/a/audre_lorde_qu.htm

Marquez, Matthew J., Monin, Benoît, Sawyer, Pamela J. "The Rejection of Moral Rebels: Resenting Those Who Do the Right Thing." *Journal of Personality and Social Psychology*. 2008, Vol. 95, No. 1, 76–93.

Maslow, A. H. "A Theory of Human Motivation." *Psychological Review*, 50, 370-396. 1943.

Maslow, Abraham H. *Motivation and Personality*. New York: Harper. 1954.

McLeod, Saul. "Maslow's Hierarchy of Needs." *Simply Psychology*. 2007. www.simplypsychology.org/maslow.html

"Nursing Fundamentals 1. Multimedia Edition - Patient Relations - Basic Human Needs and Principles of Health." Academy of Health Sciences, United States Army Medical Department, San Antonio, Texas. http://www.brooksidepress.org/Products/Nursing_Fundamentals_1/lesson_1_Section_1.htm

Pacana, Gregory. "Why we do the things we do." Human Behavior; *Examiner.com*. August 11, 2012. http://www.examiner.com/article/why-we-do-the-things-we-do

Ritholtz, Barry. *The Power of Habit: Why We Do The Things We Do*. March 10th, 2012. http://www.ritholtz.com/blog/2012/03/the-power-of-habit-why-we-do-the-things-we-do/

Ryan, Richard M., and Deci, Edward L. "Self-determination Theory and the Facilitation of Intrinsic Motivation, Social Development, and Well-being." *American Psychologist* 55.1 (2000): 68-78.

Thorndike, E. L. "Animal Intelligence: An Experimental Study of the Associative Processes in Animals." *Psychological Review* 5.5 (1898): 551-53.

BIBLIOGRAPHY

Chapter Four:
THE GOODNESS OF SELF-INTEREST

"A Raisin in the Sun" (1961). http://www.allmovie.com/movie/a-raisin-in-the-sun-v40173

Adam, Gerhard. "Self-Interest Versus Selfishness." *Science2.0.com*. July 3rd 2009. http://www.science20.com/gerhard_adam/blog/selfinterest_versus_selfishness

Adam, Gerhard. "The Virtue (?) of Selfishness." *Science2.0.com*. May 21 2009. http://www.science20.com/gerhard_Zadam/virtue_selfishness

Carter, Aaron. "Survival of the Fittest: Competition and Cooperation." Steppenwolf Theatre Company. 2011 http://www.steppenwolf.org/watchlisten/program-articles/article.aspx?id=275

De Tocqueville, Alexis. *Democracy in America*. New York: Anchor, 1969.

Eisenberg, Nancy, and Richard Fabes. "Prosocial Development." *Handbook of Child Psychology*, Vol. 3: *Social, Emotional, and Personality Development*, 5th edition. New York: John Wiley and Sons, 1998.

Eisenberg, Nancy and Paul Henry Mussen. *The Roots of Prosocial Behavior in Children*. Cambridge, UK: Cambridge University Press, 1989.

Jarrett-Karr, Nick. "Valuing and Judging Partners—Beyond the Elephant Test!" *Edge International Review*, Summer 2006.

Kangas, Olli E. "Self-interest and the common good: The impact of norms, selfishness and context in social policy opinions." *The Journal of Socio-Economics*, 26, (5), pages 475-494, 1997.

Klein, Shawn. "Community and American Individualism." *The Atlas Society*. November 2001. http://www.atlassociety.org/community-and-american-individualism

Knafo, Ariel, Weiner, Michelle, and Dubrovsky, Irit. "Proso cial Behavior." *Education.com*. http://www.education.com/reference/article/prosocial-behavior/

Kohn, Alfie. *The Brighter Side of Human Nature*. New York: Basic Books, 1992.

Larson, David. "Adam Smith: Selfishness or Self-Interest?" *Spectrum Magazine*. http://www.spectrummagazine.org/node/1368

Miller, Dale,T. "The Norm of Self Interest." *American Psychologist*, 54, (12) December 1999, 1053-1060.

Rand, A. *Atlas shrugged*. New York: Signet. 1992. (Original work published 1957).

"Self-fulfilling Prophecy." *PsychologyandSociety.com*. http://www.psychologyandsociety.com/self-fulfillingprophecy.html

Syverson, Chad. "How Productivity Benefits from Competition" *Chicago Booth News*. http://www.chicagobooth.edu/news/2007-06-15_syverson-audio.aspx

Velasquez, M., Andre, C., Shanks, T., Meyer, M. "The Common Good." *Issues in Ethics* 5, (N1), Spring 1992. http://www.scu.edu/ethics/practicing/decision/commongood.html

West, Stuart. "The Evolutionary Benefits of Cooperation: Competition Between Groups Drives Cooperation Within Groups." *BeingHuma.org*. October 10, 2012. http://www.beinghuman.org/big-questions/article/evolutionary-benefits-cooperation

Chapter Five:

"DAMN. I'VE GOTTA PEE."

Apostolides, Marianne. "The Pleasure of Pain: Find out why one in 10 of us is into S&M." *Psychology Today*. September 01, 1999.

Bernstein, W. M. A *Basic Theory of Neuropsychoanalysis*. Kar nac Books, 2011.

Dettmer, William H.; *The Logical Thinking Process: A Systems Approach to Complex Problem Solving*. American Society for Quality; 2nd edition, 2007.

Friedman, M. and L. Savage; "The Expected Utility Hypothesis and the Measurability of Utility." *Journal of Political Economy*, 60, 463-474. (1952).

Goldratt, E. M. *Theory of Constraints*. The North River Press, 1990.

Hammond, J. Daniel. "The Inexact and Separate Science of Economics." *Economics and Philosophy*. Cambridge: Cambridge University Press, 1992.

"His Cheating Brain." *Newsweek*. March 11, 2008. ttp://www.thedailybeast.com/newsweek/2008/03/12/his-cheating-brain.html

Kahneman, Daniel; Tversky, Amos. "Choices, Values, and Frames." *American Psychologist*, Volume 39(4), Apr 1984, 341-350.

MacHale, D., Sloane, P. *Intriguing Lateral Thinking Puzzles*. Sterling Publishing Company, Inc. New York. 1996.

McDonald's USA Nutrition Facts for Popular Menu Items. McDonald's Corporation. http://www.nutrition.mcdonalds.com/getnutrition/nutritionfacts.pdf.

"Methamphetamine: Highly Addictive and Highly Dangerous." The National Clearinghouse for Alcohol and Drug Information. http://www.4therapy.com/life-topics/substance-abuse/methamphetamine-highly-addictive-and-highly-dangerous-2478

NSW Government. Drug and Alcohol Facts Sheet. 01 June 2011. http://www0.health.nsw.gov.au/factsheets/drugAndAlcohol/alcohol.html

Patoine, Brenda. "Desperately Seeking Satisfaction: Fear, Reward, and the Human Need for Novelty." *The DANA Foundation*. October 2009. http://www.dana.org/media/detail.aspx?id=23620

Rawn, Moss L. "Psychoanalysis: The Impossible Profession." *Psychoanalytic Psychology* 5.1 (1988): 81-82. http://www.psychologytoday.com/articles/199909/the-pleasure-pain

"Sadomasochism." *Wikipedia.com.* http://en.wikipedia.org/wiki/Sadomasochism

Scitovsky, Tibor. "The Desire for Excitement In Modern Society." *Kyklos* 34.1 (1981): 3-13.

Snyder, C. R., Lopez, Shane J. *Positive Psychology.* Sage Publications, Inc. 2007.

Stoller, Robert J., "Sexual Excitement." *Archives of General Psychiatry.* 1976; 33(8): 899-909.

"Urinary Incontinence " Part 2—Boston Spinal Cord". *Va.gov.* 2009-11-11. Physiology of Urinaton. http://www.ouhsc.edu/geriatricmedicine/Education/Incontinence/INCONTPhysiology_of_Urination.htm

Chapter Six:
RISK

Adam, John. "Risky Business. The Management of Risk and Uncertainty." Adam Smith Institute. ASI (Research) Ltd, London. 1999.

Cherkis, Jason. "7½ Reasons Not to Have Sex in Union Station's Bathrooms: Sen. Larry Craig is alleged to have engaged in oral sex in a Union Station stall. He didn't climax. No surprise there." *Washington City Paper.* 2007. http://www.washingtoncitypaper.com/articles/2560/7-reasons-not-to-have-sex-in-union-stations-bathrooms

Grass, Michael, E."Infamous Larry Craig Men's Room Under Renovation." *Washington City Paper.* September 20, 2010. http://www.washingtoncitypaper.com/blogs/citydesk/2010/09/20/infamous-larry-craig-mens-room-under-renovation/

Horvath, P., Zuckerman, M. "Sensation Seeking." *Personality and Individual Differences.* Volume 14, Issue 1, January

1993, Pages 41–52.

Weber, Bethany J., Chapman, Gretchen B.; "Playing for peanuts: Why is risk seeking more common for low-stakes gambles?" *Organizational Behavior and Human Decision Processes*; Volume 97, Issue 1, May 2005, Pages 31–46.

Zuckerman, Marvin. "Are You a Risk Raker?" *Psychology Today*. Nov/Dec 2000. http://cms.psychologytoday.com/articles/index.php?term=pto-20001101-000035.x... 7/13/2005.

Zuckerman, Marvin and Michael Kuhlman. "Personality and Risk-Taking: Common Biosocial Factors." *Journal of Personality*. 68: 6, December 2000.

Zuckerman, M.; "Sensation Seeking and Risky Behavior." *American Psychological Association*. 2007.

Chapter Seven
CHOCOLATE PEPPERS

Baldwin, James. *Collected Essays*. New York: Library of America, 1998.

Barnett, Christopher F. and De Marco, Teresa. "A chocolate a day keeps the doctor away?" *Journal of Physiology*. December 2011; 5921-5922(24): 5921-5922.

Benelam, B. "Satiation, Satiety and Their Effects on Eating Behaviour." *Nutrition Bulletin* 34.2 (2009): 126-73.

Berridge, KC., Ho, Chao-Yi, Richard, JM., DiFeliceantonio, AG., "The tempted brain eats: Pleasure and desire circuits in obesity and eating disorders." *Brain Research*, Volume 1350, 2 September 2010, Pages 43-64.

"Chocolate: The Psychoactive Cocktail." http://www.chocolate.org/

Cooper, K., Donovan, J. Waterhouse, A., Williamson, G. "Cocoa and Health: a decade of research." *British Journal of Nutrition*. January 2008; 1-11(1).

Finlayson, G., N. King, and J. Blundell. "Is It Possible to Dissociate 'liking' and 'wanting' for Foods in Humans? A Novel Experimental Procedure." *Physiology & Behavior*

90.1 (2007): 36-42.
"Global hunger declining, but still unacceptably high; International hunger targets difficult to reach." *Food and Agriculture Organization of the United Nations. Economic and Social Development Department.* September 2010.
Holy Bible: 1611 Edition : King James Version. Peabody, MA: Hendrickson, 2003.
The Holy Bible: New International Version. Colorado Springs, CO: International Bible Society, 1984.
"Infant Masturbation Often Misdiagnosed." *LiveScience.* (2005). http://www.livescience.com/3957-infant-masturbation-misdiagnosed.html
Kancigor, Judy, B. "Chocolate—so much to learn and taste-test." *Orange County Register.* March, 2013. http://www.ocregister.com/news/chocolate-498529-food-cookbook.html
Kroll, Luisa. "Inside The 2013 Billionaires List: Facts and Figures." *Forbes.* Forbes Magazine, 04 Mar. 2013.
Langer, S., Marshall L.J., Day A.J., Morgan M.R.; "Flavanols and Methylxanthines in Commercially-available Dark Chocolate: A Study of the Correlation With Non-fat Cocoa Solids." *Journal of Agricultural and Food Chemistry.* July 2011.
Levine, Carrie. "Sexuality & fertility. Health benefits of self-cultivation." *Women to Women.* (2011). http://www.womentowomen.com/sexualityandfertility/healthbenefitsofmasturbation.aspx
Maimonides, Moses, and M. Friedlander. *The Guide for the Perplexed.* London: G. Routledge & Sons, 1910.
McShea, A., Ramiro-Puig, E., Munro, S., Casadesus, G., Castell, M., Smith, M. "Clinical benefit and preservation of flavonols in dark chocolate manufacturing." *Nutrition Reviews.* November 2008; 630-641(11): 630-641.
Micronutrient Deficiency: A Global Challenge to Health. The World Health Organization. 2002. http://www.iaea.org/

newscenter/features/nutrition/micronutrient.html

"MLE." *Major League Eating & International Federation of Competitive Eating.* http://www.ifoce.com/contests.php

Phipps, William E. "Masturbation: Vice or Virtue?" *Journal of Religion & Health* 16.3 (1977): 183-95.

"Resources for Speakers, Global Issues, Africa, Ageing, Agriculture, Aids, Atomic Energy, Children, Climate Change, Culture, Decolonization, Demining, Development, Disabilities, Disarmament, Environment, Food, Governance, Humanitarian, Refugees, Women." *UN News Center.* UN, n.d. http://www.un.org/en/globalissues/briefingpapers/food/whatishunger.shtml

Slaughter, Gwen. "Is Chocolate Physiologically or Psychologically Addictive?" *Serendip. BrynMawr.edu.* Bryn Mawr College. 2001. http://serendip.brynmawr.edu/bb/neuro/neuro01/web2/Slaughter.html

Stoppler, Melissa, C. "Endorphins: Natural Pain and Stress Fighters." *MedicineNet.com.* http://www.medicinenet.com/script/main/art.asp?articlekey=55001

Stuart, Annie. "Peppers and Your Health. A look at the potential health benefits that peppers may hold." *WebMD.* October 5, 2010.

Taubert, Dirk; Roesen, Renate; Lehmann, Clara; Jung, Norma; Schömig, Edgar. "Effects of Low Habitual Cocoa Intake on Blood Pressure and Bioactive Nitric OxideA Randomized Controlled Trial." *JAMA,* July 4, 2007—Vol 298, No. 1. http://www.webmd.com/food-recipes/features/health-benefits-of-peppers

"Why Are We Hungry? Part I: What Is Hunger? Liking Vs. Wanting, Satiation Vs. Satiety." *Gnolls.org.* July, 2011. http://www.gnolls.org/2304/why-are-we-hungry-part-1-what-is-hunger-liking-vs-wanting-satiation-vs-satiety/

Yap, Lauren. "Chocolate and history displayed at museum exhibit." *The Daily Aztec.* March 06, 2013. http://www.thedailyaztec.com/2013/03/chocolate-and-history-displayed-at-museum-exhibit/

BIBLIOGRAPHY

Chapter Eight:
THE PEPPER TREE

Diekstra, R. F. W. *Suicide and Its Prevention: The Role of Attitude and Imitation*. Leiden: E.J. Brill, 1989.
"DrugFacts: Comorbidity: Addiction and Other Mental Disorders." *National Institute on Drug Abuse*. March 2011. http://www.drugabuse.gov/publications/drugfacts/comorbidity-addiction-other-mental-disorders
Gabriel, Satya J. *"Oliver Stone's Wall Street and the Market for Corporate Control. Economics in Popular Film."* Mount Holyoke. 2001.
Hanes, Richard Clay, Sharon M. Hanes, Kelly Rudd, and Sarah Hermsen. *Crime and Punishment in America*. Detroit: UXL, 2005.
Harris, Sam. *Lying*. Four Elephants Press, 2013.
"Just How Many Spouses Cheat? Karlyn Bowman. Everything you ever wanted to know about extramarital sex—and whether it matters." *Forbes Magazine*, 2009. http://www.forbes.com/2009/06/28/sanford-ensign-affair-opinions-columnists-extramarital-sex.html
Kahneman, Daniel, and Amos Tversky. *Choices, Values, and Frames*. New York: Russell Sage Foundation, 2000.
LaBier, Douglas. "Having An Affair? There Are Six Different Kinds. Affairs come in an array of flavors." *The New Resilience*, 2010/. http://www.psychologytoday.com/blog/the-new-resilience/201004/having-affair-there-are-six-different-kinds
Oliver, Richard, L. "A Cognitive Model of the Antecedents and Consequences of Satisfaction Decisions." *Journal of Marketing Research*. Vol. 17, No. 4 (1980), pp. 460-469.
Ostler, Scott. "Captain Spree should remain a landlubber". *The San Francisco Chronicle*. January 8, 2011.
Schwartz, Mel. "Looking at Greed as an Addictive Dysfunction. We are a society that is addicted to abundance and

extravagance." *Psychology Today*. (2008). http://www.psychologytoday.com/blog/shift-mind/200812/looking-greed-addictive-dysfunction

"Skydiver and base jumper, Valery Rozov, talks about his passion for flight and his journey to a world record." *Sunday Times*. March 17, 2013. http://www.sundaytimes.lk/analysisinterviews/31475-skydiver-and-base-jumper-valery-rozov-talks-about-his-passion-for-flight-and-his-journey-to-a-world-record.html

Smiley, Jane. "Morality; The Good Lie." *The New York Times Magazine*. May 07, 2000.
http://www.nytimes.com/2000/05/07/magazine/morality-the-good-lie.html?pagewanted=all&src=pm

"Stress Symptoms: Effects on Your Body, Feelings and Behavior." *Mayo Clinic*. Mayo Foundation for Medical Education and Research, 19 Feb. 2011. http://www.mayoclinic.com/health/stress-symptoms/SR00008_D

Willman, David. "Premier Rock Climber Falls to His Death in Yosemite : Accident: Derek Hersey Was a Free-soloist, Using No Ropes or Equipment. A Friend Says He May Have Encountered Moisture and Slipped on Sentinel Rock." *Los Angeles Times*. Los Angeles Times, 31 May 1993.
http://articles.latimes.com/1993-05-31/news/mn-41958_1_sentinel-rock

Chapter Nine:
5 TIPS FOR ENJOYING YOURSELF
AND BEING BETTER

Bernstein, Jeffrey. "Liking the Child You Love." *Psychology Today*. December 18, 2010. http://www.psychologytoday.com/blog/liking-the-child-you-love/201012/the-two-real-causes-misery

Edwards, Tab. *I&O Strategy: Imaging & Output Strategy*.
Philadelphia: Oxford Hill Press. 2011.

Lorde, Audre. *Sister Outsider: Essays and Speeches*. Freedom,

CA.: Crossing Press. 1984.

Chapter Ten:
THE CHAIN OF SELF-INTERESTLINKED:
A SUMMARY

Layton, Julia. "How Fear Works." 13 September 2005. HowStuffWorks.com.http://science.howstuffworks.com/life/fear.htm.

Posner, Roy. "From Reluctance to Acceptance to the Pinnacles of Success." *Human Science*. http://humanscience.wikia.com/wiki/From_Reluctance_to_Acceptance_to_the_Pinnacles_of_Success. 1 May 2009.

Svoboda, Elizabeth. "Field Guide to the People-Pleaser: May I Serve as Your Doormat? Why are some people so focused on pleasing others that they sacrifice their own needs?" *Psychology Today*. May 01, 2008. http://www.psychologytoday.com/articles/200805/field-guide-the-people-pleaser-may-i-serve-your-doormat.

CONCLUSION

Hemingway, Ernest. *The Sun Also Rises*. New York: Scribner, 1996.

INDEX

Symbols

5 Tips for Enjoying Yourself and Being Better 222

A

ABC-Wide-World-of-Sports 149
Abraham Maslow 24, 70, 174
 A Theory of Human Motivation 24, 70, 174, 270
 physical needs 70
 Maslow 24, 25, 56, 70, 71, 72, 73, 75, 77, 84, 99, 132, 174, 199, 270
 Motivation and Personality 70, 270
 Theory of Human Motivation 24, 70, 174
  hierarchy of needs 25, 70, 190
  being need, or B-needs 71
  deficiency needs, or D-needs 71
  love, and general affection 71
  physical needs 70
  safety 15, 16, 26, 70, 71, 74, 99, 127, 136, 146, 180, 259
  safety and security 70
  self-actualization 56, 71, 72, 74, 100, 109, 199, 215, 216, 232, 234, 252, 262
  self-esteem need 25, 74
  Types of Needs 73–77
Absolutism 179
abusive relationship 26
actions 16, 17, 55, 58, 62, 68, 77, 78, 82, 83, 84, 85, 86, 88, 101, 111, 112, 116, 118, 120, 121, 124, 126, 127, 128, 133, 149, 155, 189, 193, 196, 197, 199, 200, 228, 246, 251, 254
Actions 118, 127, 128, 246
acupuncture 141
Adam Smith 83, 86, 101, 103, 255, 272, 274
 It is not from the benevolence of the butcher, the brewer, or the baker 103–295, 256–295
Airlines Flight 15
airplane 15, 16, 17, 33, 77, 260
alcohol addiction 18, 18, 18, 19
Alek Wek 43
Alexis de Tocqueville 89
 Democracy in America 89
allup poll 200
Amancio Ortega 158
American Economic Review 41, 267
Amos Tversky 178, 278
Annie Jones 23
Apple 91

INDEX

apple pie 133
approval of others 22, 25
A Raisin in the Sun 82, 271
Aristotle 46
   Personal beauty is a better introduction than any letter 46
Arthur "The Fonz" Fonzarelli 66
"A" then "B" 111, 149
A Theory of Human Motivation 24, 70, 174, 270
attractive, 39, 40, 41, 42, 204
Audre Lorde 246, 270
Ayn Rand 104–295, 104
  good of the majority 104

B

baclofen 18
Barbara Billingsley 260
Barry Manilow 138, 244
BASE-jumping 155, 187
bathe 21, 22, 23
  bathing 22, 87
beauty is in the eye of the beholder 43
Being Better: An Abbreviated Five Stage Strategy 231
Being Better: A Strategy for Enjoying Yourself and Leading a More Fulfilling, Less Miserable Life 222
  5 Tips for Enjoying Yourself and Being Better 222
Being Bobby Brown 80
being need, or B-needs 71
Bible 135, 137, 276
  Genesis 137
  New International Version of the Bible 137
Big Bank Hank 240
  The Sugar Hill Gang 240
Bill Gates 158
Bobby Brown 80
Bobby's Got the Munchies 206
Brad Pitt 43, 45
Brooks Brothers 64, 66, 69
Buddhist monks 77
business suit 21, 29
Buy the shoes and eat the chocolate 50

C

Carlos Slim 158
Catherine Kaputa 40
  perceived attractiveness 40
Catholicism 26
  Catholics 26
  divorce 26, 217
causation 111
cause-and-effect 111
Chad Syverson 92
Chain of Self-Interest 34, 251
Channing Tatum 194
Charles Darwin 92
  natural selection 92
chili pepper 162–171
Chocolate 5–14, 9–18, 160–170, 275–287
  food of the gods 5–14, 9–18, 160–170, 275–287
Chocolate Peppers 156–170, 275–289
Chris Rock 158
Christian Children's Fund (ChildFund) 78
Christians 135
Civil Libertarians 188
coincidence 111, 112
Common Good 102
  hunter-gatherers 102
  John Rawls 102–295
common sense 108, 115, 125, 190

INDEX

conformity 24
conundrum 141
  Masochism 141
cooperation 39, 41, 78, 89, 91, 92, 95, 101, 104, 105, 255, 272
Cornell University 18
Coulrophobia (the fear of clowns) 229
  hypothesis of the "Valley" 229
crack-heads 184
credibility 39
Creme Brulee 125
crystal meth 188
Cultural taboos 138
  masturbation 138
Current Biology 24
  conformity 24, 67
  social conformity 24
Curtis 'Miles' Armstrong 31

D

Daisy Cottage Cheese 164
Dale T. Miller 88
"Damn. I've Gotta Pee!" 106, 272
Damn! I wish I woulda 25, 27, 30
Daniel Gilbert 54
Daniel Kahneman 57
  experiencing self 57
  remembering self 57
Decision-making 86, 107, 112, 116, 118, 126, 133, 140, 146, 150, 155, 165, 166, 167, 189, 227, 241, 253, 254
  Decision-Making Model 117
  Decision-Support Tool 166, 169
Decision-Support Tool 166, 169
deficiency needs, or D-needs 71
Dell 91
Democracy in America 89, 271

Demonstration 15
Derek Geoffrey 186
descriptions of "happiness" 84
Dice man 147
differentiators between selfishness and self-interest 83
  sympathy 83
Disney World 239
Divorce 26, 217
Do Diddly Day 245
dominatrix 142, 143
Do Something 233
Douglas LaBier 201
Drew Carey 23
  Whose Line is it Anyway? 23
  wash our hands 23, 24
Drug addiction 190

E

Eating contests 157
  Wing Bowl 157
economic prosperity 33
Ed Diener 57, 84, 268
  descriptions of "happiness" 84
Edward Thorndike 65
  The Law of Effect 65
elimination 113
empathy 101
Endorphins 161
Engagement 56
Ernest Hemingway 259
Euphoria 161, 161–295
Eva Mendes 43
Example of "Self-Interest" 86, 87
  Manolo Blahnik 87
Example of "Selfish" 86, 87
Expected Effects 128
expected outcome 111, 116
Expected Utility Theory 150
  probability 118, 150, 215, 216, 252, 253

INDEX

Experienced happiness 57
experiencing self 57
external influence 26, 28, 133, 191, 193, 194, 262
extramarital affair 200
   having an affair can be psychologically healthy 204
   six kinds of affairs 201
extrinsic reason 62

F

Fear
   Fight or flight 226
   The Role of Fear 225
      survival of the species 88, 92, 146, 226
Fight or flight 226
flight attendant 15, 260
Flourish: A Visionary New Understanding of Happiness and Well-being 56
food of the gods 160
Force Yourself to be Happy 239
   Guilty-Pleasure List 239
   Rule of 41 239
Fortune 500® corporation 31
Foxconn 91
Frank Serpico 66
Fred G. Sanford 64, 69
   pea-green sweater 64, 66, 69
free-solo 186, 187, 188, 192

G

Gallup poll 200
   external influence 200
Gerhard Adam 84
Goals. 126
GOD Delusion 135
GODs Model
   Do Something 231, 233, 235

high school reunion 126, 128, 231, 233, 234, 235
   Objective 232
      S.M.A.R.T. 232
   Strategy 222, 230, 234, 238, 263, 280
good-for-me-good-for-others-too 17
good-looking 41, 42
   attractive 39, 40, 41, 42, 204
   beautiful 27, 29, 30, 32, 41, 42, 44, 46, 268
good of the majority 104
greater good 20
guilt 31, 138, 139, 142, 198, 199, 200, 202, 211, 225, 228, 254, 263
Guilty-Pleasure List 241, 242, 243, 244, 245, 263

H

Hakuho Sho 173
happiness 25, 34, 35, 38, 39, 49–68, 50, 52, 53, 54, 55–74, 57, 58, 59, 75, 84, 85, 88, 89, 90, 139, 161, 168, 170, 186, 187, 190, 193, 195, 204, 205, 211, 212, 217, 223, 230, 239, 240, 243, 245, 246, 247, 254, 255, 260, 261, 269
   descriptions of "happiness" 84
   three degrees of separation 59, 254
happiness can spread to others 59
Happiness Impact 193
happiness-interrupters 59
happy 20–264
   happiness 25—259
Harper's Bazaar 23
Harris Interactive 23

INDEX

HBO 158
  Chris Rock 158
heroin 188
Hewlett-Packard 91, 265
hierarchy of needs 25, 70, 190
"How'd He Get HER?!" 43
H-P 91
humans are predominantly self-interested 88
hunter-gatherers 102
hypothesis of the "Valley" 229

I

ignorance 108, 122, 123
Impact on others 204
individualism 88, 89, 90, 272
individualistically 88
In-Flight Safety 15
In Living Color 106
  Keenen Ivory Wayans 106
  Ted Turner's Colorized Classics 106
intrinsic 62, 68, 69, 84, 109, 134, 151, 152, 159, 262
intrinsic curiosity 109
intrinsic reason 62
invisible ball & chain 197, 200
irrational 77, 79, 125, 131, 153, 199, 224
  irrational thought 125
Islam 135
It is not from the benevolence of the butcher, the brewer, or the baker 103–295, 256–295

J

James Baldwin 135
James Dean 66
James Fowler 59

Jean Shrimpton 43
Jeffrey Bernstein 224
Jehovah's Witness 112
John Adams 147
  Dice man 147
  Zero-risk man 147, 147
Johnny Carson 167
John Rawls 102
joy 53
joyful 52
J.R.R. Tolkien 181
Judaism 135, 248

K

Keenen Ivory Wayans 106
Keeping up with the Joneses 248
Keynote Speaker 31
Ku Klux Klan 248

L

Larry Craig 154, 155, 274
laws 191
LeBron James 196, 197, 225
Lene Gammelgaard 48
Letter to a Christian Nation 135
Liking 159, 277, 280
Linda Tillman 246
logic 38, 125, 126, 127, 132, 135, 183, 243
  Logical thinking 125
Long-term happiness 58
Lorraine Hansberry 82
  A Raisin in the Sun 82, 271
Lying 96
  Lying can take many forms 96
  Resplying 99

M

Madonna 66
Major League Eating 158, 277

Malcolm X 66
man is basically ignorant 108
Manolo Blahnik 87
Man on Wire 151
Margaret Wolfe Hungerford 43
  Molly Bawn 43
    beauty is in the eye of the beholder 43
Mark of the Devil 153, 154
Marlboro Light 82
Martin Seligman
  Flourish: A Visionary New Understanding of Happiness and Well-being 56
  Positive psychology 56
Maslow 24, 25, 56, 70, 71, 72, 73, 75, 77, 84, 99, 132, 174, 199, 270
Masochism 141
  sadomasochism 142
masturbation 137–146, 138–147, 139–148, 276–285
  badger the witness 139
  box the bald-headed clown 139
  fire the Surgeon-General 139
  Jill off 139
  Mork the Mindy 139
  Pat the Robertson 139
  slap-box the one-eyed champ 139
  smoke hooch with Reagan 139
  torture the political prisoner 139
  verb the noun 139, 238
  wave the writ of Habeas Corpus to the Sheriff of Nottingham 140
Meaning 56, 269
men's suit 27
  $5,000 Suit 29, 267
  business suit 21, 29
mentally sane 108, 115, 190

Methamphetamine 128, 273
  crystal meth 188
  Ice 128, 158
  Speed 128
Michelin PAX tires 50
Mike Tyson 214, 215, 216, 217
Miserable 222, 223, 230
  misery 223, 224, 230, 237, 280
  Misery Avoidance Tip 237, 238
  pitfalls of being miserable 224
Molly Bawn 43
Moses Maimonides 136
Motivation and Personality 70, 270
movie Airplane 260
Mr. T 94
My Inner-Self 30

N

National Basketball Association 224
  NBA's Development League 224
National Football League 196
National Institute on Alcohol Abuse and Alcoholism 18
National Institute on Drug Abuse 190
natural selection 92
New International Version of the Bible 137
Nicholas Christakis 59
Nosferatu 239
nothing-to-do-Saturday 21, 22, 23
  shave 23, 24
    objectionable hair 23
    underarm hair 23

O

Objective 232

INDEX

S.M.A.R.T. 232
Olivier Ameisen 18, 19, 33
  alcohol addiction 18
  The End of My Addiction 18, 267
  opinions of us 22, 23, 24, 25, 63
  our actions are based on positive payoffs and rewards 88
  overall general attractiveness 40
oxygen mask 16, 17, 259, 260
Ozwald Boateng 45

P

packaging 32, 40, 43
  overall general attractiveness 40
PAIN 133
Pancho Villa 67
Paul "Pee-Wee Herman" Reubens 194
pea-green sweater 64, 66, 69
peanuts effect 154
pee 113, 114
people-pleasers 246
people's perceptions of acting self-interested 93
Pepper Tree 10, 155, 164, 166, 167, 169, 170, 173, 176, 178, 179, 183, 185, 189, 192, 194, 201, 203, 204, 205, 206, 208, 212, 214, 219, 220, 240, 241, 243, 244, 253, 261, 262
  Decision-Support Tool 166, 169
    Pepper Tree Work Chart 169
    The Pepper Tree Work Chart Elements 172
Pepper Tree Work Chart 169–22
  Bobby's Got the Munchies 206
  Mike Tyson 214, 215, 216, 217
  Mitch "Blood" Green 217
  The Pepper Tree Work Chart Elements 172
perceived attractiveness 40
permanently happy 53, 58
Personal beauty is a better introduction than any letter 46
Peter Paul Rubens 42
Philadelphia 6, 15, 46, 157, 268, 280
physical needs 70
Pigs' Feet 125
pimp-slap your enemy 198
pitfalls of being miserable 224
Pleasure 56–243
pleasure principle 140
pleasure-seekers 193
pork 134, 135, 136, 137
Positive psychology 54
  happiness 54–73
pot of beans 37
probability 118, 150, 215, 216, 252, 253
Problem Resolution 116
Prosocial Behavior 100
psychopath 199
P. T. Barnum 23
P.T. Barnum
  Annie Jones 23
Public Interest 102

R

R3 107
Rachel Bachner-Melman 80
Rational 107, 108, 110, 112, 114, 115, 118, 122, 125, 129, 189, 233, 241, 247
  mentally sane 108, 115, 190
  rationality 132, 135, 146, 155
Rationality 190
Rational Routing Routine 107

INDEX

decision-making 86, 107, 112, 116, 118, 126, 133, 140, 146, 150, 155, 165, 166, 167, 189, 227, 241, 253, 254
  man is basically ignorant 108
  wilderness vacation 108
R3 107, 110, 112, 113, 115, 116, 117, 120, 122, 125, 129, 189
Rational 107, 108, 110, 112, 114, 115, 118, 122, 125, 129, 189, 233, 241, 247
resolving a problem 111, 116, 117
riddle 108, 109, 122, 123, 124, 167
Routine 107, 110, 113, 114, 115, 116, 118, 122, 125, 129, 189, 233, 241
  Problem Resolution 116, 116
  Urinating 114
Routing 107, 110, 111, 112, 114, 115, 116, 118, 122, 125, 129, 189, 233, 241
  "A" then "B" 111, 149
  cause-and-effect 111
    causation 111
    coincidence 111, 112
reality principle 134
rebel 66, 67
Reference experience 184
  crack-heads 184
relative 125, 141, 169, 179, 209, 215, 219, 262
Relativism 179
relief 52, 53, 114, 161
religious customs 26
Religious restrictions 135
  pork 134, 135, 136, 137
    trichinosis 136
remembering self 57
Remorse 198
requency of satisfying events 245
resolving a problem 111, 116, 117
Resplying 99
Richard Dawkins 135
  GOD Delusion 135
riddle 108, 109, 122, 123, 124, 167
  speakeasy 122
  Why did an old lady always answer the door wearing her hat and coat? 109
Risk 145, 274
  BASE-jumping 155, 187
  peanuts effect 154
  risk-accepters 147
  risk assessment 149
  risk-avoiders 147
  risk-seeker 147
    Man on Wire 151
    stimulus deficit 143, 151, 154, 185, 186
  risk-taking 146, 147, 152, 153
    risk-takers 147, 148
  risky behavior 146
risk-accepters 147
risk assessment 149
risk-avoiders 146, 147, 148
risk-seeker 147
risk-taking 146, 147, 152, 153
  Larry Craig 154, 155, 274
  stimulus deficit 143, 151, 154, 185, 186
risky behavior 146
risky behavior, 146
Risky Business 31, 274
  Curtis 'Miles' Armstrong 31
  what the f**k 31, 50, 220
Robots 67–295

INDEX

Robots and Rebels 66
Routine 107, 110, 113, 114, 115, 116, 118, 122, 125, 129, 189, 233, 241
 Problem Resolution 116
Routing 107, 110, 111, 112, 114, 115, 116, 118, 122, 125, 129, 189, 233, 241
Roy Baumeister 142
 Masochism 142
Rule of 41 240, 243, 254

S

sadomasochism 142
 dominatrix 142, 143
 S&M 142, 143, 155, 273
safety and security 70
Salli Richardson 43
Sally Struthers 78
 Christian Children's Fund (ChildFund) 78
Sam Harris 100, 135
 Letter to a Christian Nation 135
Satisfaction 74–83, 118–127, 181–190, 183–192, 254–263, 273–282, 279–288
Science 2.0 84
 Gerhard Adam 84
self-actualization 56, 71, 72, 74, 100, 109, 199, 215, 216, 232, 234, 252, 262
self-determination 69
self-determined 68, 69
self-esteem need 25, 74
self-fulfilling prophecy 95
Self-Interest 34–63, 76–105, 81–110, 93–122, 251–280, 271–300
 humans are predominantly self-interested 88

Selfishness vs. Self-Interest 81
 empathy 101
selfless 76, 78, 79, 80
Selflessness 76–105
Seventh-day Adventists 135
Shawn E. Klein 89
Shel Silverstein 79
 The Giving Tree 79
Shemar Moore 43
Sidney Poitier 82
Sigmund Freud 140
 pleasure principle 140
six kinds of affairs 201
S&M 142, 143, 155, 273
S.M.A.R.T. 232
Sonja Lyubomirsky 55
Sophia Loren 43
Steve McQueen 66
stimulation 186
stimulus deficit 143, 151, 154, 185, 186
Strategy 222, 230, 234, 238, 263, 280
suicide 191
Super Bowl XLVII 61
supposition 20, 33, 100
survival of the species 88, 92, 146, 226
Swiss 162
switch 62, 63–62, 65, 66–65, 111, 112–111
sympathy 83

T

Tab Edwards 5, 6, 13, 13, 265
 Keynote Speaker 31
  Fortune 500® corporation 31
Ted Turner's Colorized Classics 106
Tetrahydrocannabinol (THC) 161
The Chain of Self-Interest 10, 33,

34, 37
The Dating Game 45
The Giving Tree 79
The GOD Delusion 135
The Goodness of Self-Interest 9, 34
The Hobbit 181–183
The Journal of Economic Psychology 41
  cooperation 39, 41, 78, 89, 91, 92, 95, 101, 104, 105, 255, 272
The Law of Effect 65
Theory of Human Motivation 24, 70, 174, 270
The Pepper Tree 166
The Public Interest 102
The Role of Fear 225
The Spread of Happiness 59
The Stigma of Self-Interest 93
The Sugar Hill Gang 240
Thiekthou, Southern Sudan 158
three degrees of separation 59, 254
Tim 44, 45, 46, 47, 48
  Ugly Tim 44, 45, 46, 47
Tonight Show 167
  Johnny Carson 167
trichinosis 136
Types of Needs 73–77

U

Ugly Tim 44, 45, 46, 47
Unfulfilled Needs 126
University of Illinois 75
Urinating 114

V

Value 24, 25, 96, 110, 115, 121–125, 123, 149, 150

Verb the Noun 134, 238
Verbing the Noun 130, 134
Vinko-Bogataj 149

W

Wanting 159, 277
Warren Buffett 158
what the f**k 31, 50, 220
Whitney Houston 80
Whose Line is it Anyway? 23
Why did an old lady always answer the door wearing her hat and coat? 109
Why Did I Buy That Suit? 61, 269
wilderness vacation 108
Wing Bowl 157
Wolfe Hungerford 43

Y

Yogurt 162–171, 164–173

Z

Zero-risk man 147
zero-sum game 90, 240

www.ingramcontent.com/pod-product-compliance
Lightning Source LLC
Chambersburg PA
CBHW051647040426
42446CB00009B/1011